Dedicated Dads:
Stepfathers
of Famous People

by Rusty Hancock

Lawells Publishing
Royal Oak, Michigan
2004

Great Families series

Warm and Wonderful Stepmothers of Famous People
Dedicated Dads: Stepmothers of Famous People
Fantastic Famous Stepparents
Great Grandparents of Famous People
Great Aunts of Famous People
Great Mothers-in-Law of Famous People
Illustrious Illegitimates
and more to come

- - - - - - - - - - - - -

Copyrights: text: Rusty Hancock, 2004
illustration: Megan Van Kampen, 2004
cover design: Dengate Design, 2004
cover art: Megan Van Kampen, Dengate Design

Publisher: Lawells Publishing
PO Box 1338
Royal Oak MI 48068-1338
www.lawells.net
Printed by: Sheridan Books, Ann Arbor, Michigan

PUBLISHER'S CATALOGUING IN PUBLICATION DATA
Hancock, Rusty
Dedicated dads: stepfathers of famous people / Rusty Hancock.
Twenty-seven stepfathers and the well-known people they guided, in contrast to the stereotypes of the fairy tale stepmothers of Cinderella and Hansel and Gretel and others of stepfathers. Dedicated to the author's stepmother.
illus.
ISBN 0-934981-12-4
1. Stepfamilies.   306.874
2. Biographies--miscellany. 920.02

I. Title.

L.C.No. 2004102170

Dedication

*To the memory of
Emily M. Hancock, my stepmother,
who gave a whole new meaning to
being treated "like a stepchild."*

Foreword

This is meant to be a companion book of sorts to the book that started this series: *Warm and Wonderful Stepmothers of Famous People,* dedicated to my stepmother. She was the inspiration for that one that led to this one and to an entire series dedicated to the appreciation of special people in our lives.

The titles of these two books are illustrative of the difference in roles, or how they are perceived, between men and women through the years and across the cultures. Women are still, for the most part, the nurturers.

Men as fathers are most often concerned with financially supportingand educating the next generation and guiding it in choosing a life's work. The stepfathers in here generally followed that tradition.

However, with rare exceptions, a major problem facing these men is that they are in the unsavory position of being an interloper, intruding upon the possessive relationship of children with the only biological parent who, for the most part, has remained with them. The wisest ones rode it through, ultimately came to have a good relationship with the former foe, and made it into this book.

One other constant is that these mothers seem not to have interfered with the relationship between their children and the stepfathers. The lack of a united front is harmful, to say the least, to any parenting relationship and to the marital relationship that can be its solid foundation.

With personal appreciation--and best wishes--to you all.

Sherry A. Wells

Acknowledgements

Again, to those mentioned in the previous book, who made the daunting research far easier and more thorough.

To Rusty Hancock, who authored this book, for getting so into this project that she even procured a recording by John Lee Hooker for the wonderful anecdotes in the liner notes. That is merely one example of her going beyond the assignment.

To our mutual friend, Linda, for encouragement and humor.

Contents

Dedication
Foreword
Acknowledgements

Peter Pelham, stepfather of

JOHN COPLEY, portrait painter, born circa 1738

"The most important act of Pelham's life was opening to [John Copley] the door of his workroom." James Thomas Flexner, biographer

But for his stepfather, it is doubtful that John Copley would have gained a reputation as Colonial America's most outstanding artist. He was born probably not long after his parents arrived from Ireland in 1736 and set up a tobacco shop on Boston's Long Wharf. By the time John was ten, his father had died, and his widowed mother, Mary became the administrator of his father's estate.

In 1748, she married Peter Pelham, a London-born portrait artist and engraver, who apparently left a thriving career to emigrate to America. No one is quite sure why he would have abandoned such a lucrative profession, so it may have been under questionable circumstances. It is certain that he arrived in Boston in 1727 bearing a portrait he had painted of the Governor of Massachusetts as his professional credentials. At the time of their marriage, Pelham was fifty-three and had been married twice before.

In Colonial times, one did not get to be a painter of portraits (or of any other kind of art) in a way that would be familiar today. There were no art schools, no scholarships, no inspiring movies about the life of Jackson Pollock or Gilbert Stuart. People became painters almost by accident, frequently starting out at another trade altogether, perhaps gradually branching out into related trades as the need arose in the small, isolated communities of the day. A combination of talent and local interest might lead to a carpenter taking up sign painting, and then perhaps a different type of art.

Decorative art was usually imported into the Colonies from abroad, but as portraits actually required the presence of their subject, the art of portraiture became a prospering American art form. A portrait was considered a mark of success, and in the pre-Polaroid days, it was the only way to let relatives in Europe follow the progress of families who had emigrated to the Colonies. The level of expertise in these portraits, however, was quite low, thus leaving a lot of room for a truly skilled portrait artist such as John Copley to stand out from the rest.

Peter Pelham's greatest skill was not portraiture, but rather engraving, a secondary art and means of popularizing the works of the portrait artists themselves. Although he was able to produce his own original art, Pelham preferred to reproduce the artwork of other, better-known artists, as their name and fame would make his engravings more salable. His task was to copy the original and transfer it to a metal piece, etching the picture with acid or scraping tools. Then a press would transfer the ink from the tiny acid wells to paper. Pelham's problem was finding interesting enough subjects that people would want to buy copies of them, easier done in England than in sparsely populated America. There were correspondingly few portrait painters, sometimes leaving Pelham to depend upon his own painting skills.

The Copleys had been living in three rooms atop the tobacco shop, but Pelham moved them away to a more suitable and quiet neighborhood, into "one of the few households in all the Colonies where art was the predominant interest. . .," although his wife continued to sell "the best Virginia Tobacco, Cut, Pigtail, and spun, of all sorts, by Wholesale, or Retail, at the Cheapest Rates." The neighborhood was nicer, but money was still a concern, even though Pelham had formed a partnership with local artist John Smibert, who painted the portraits which Pelham then engraved. Pelham decided to branch out. In 1732 he opened a dancing school at his house, which, as part of its curriculum, offered a monthly "assembly" of music and dance. The *Boston Gazette* immediately branded him a sinner, who was "hastening the ruin of our Country," and was well-known "Corrupter of Manners, and. . .[promoter of] Vice and Irregularities."

Nevertheless, the assemblies continued.

By 1738 he was running a school in which he taught "Dancing, Writing, Reading, Painting on Glass, and all sorts of needle work." In 1748 he established what may have been the first night school in the country, offering more limited basic business skills, such as writing and arithmetic, in response to the needs of a city that was becoming "the rapidly rising commercial capital of New England."

When John Copley arrived on the scene, a home school was ready and waiting for him, as well as an apprenticeship at the engraver's trade, alongside Pelham's two sons, who were still living at home.

Pelham had great knowledge of contemporary English artwork as well as a large collection of engravings, all of which he shared with Copley. In addition, the stepfather's friends and fellow artists all lived and worked in the neighborhood, and Copley was able to visit their studios as well. He had three brief years in which to absorb all he could about the world of painting and engraving before Peter Pelham died. Pelham's friend and partner, John Smibert. also died in 1751. The others, including Pelham's sons, all left the area for their own reasons. At thirteen, Copley was left to help support his mother and younger brother Henry.

Unlike Pelham, Copley was far more interested in painting than engraving. At first, he tried his hand at projects that were far too ambitious for his talent, although they showed promise that would later make him the leading American painter in the

3

ornate, asymmetrical Rococo style. He soon realized that the market in Boston was not interested in classical gods and nymphs, but the more practical and close-to-home art of portraiture.

Desiring money, fame, and social position, Copley evolved a style that distinguished him from all the others, and by the time he was twenty-one, he was recognized as the leading portraitist in the Colonies, able to produce a realism seldom before seen. This may have been due in part to a perfectionist nature that led him to require fifteen or more sittings for a single portrait. He also frequently employed a Rococo device known as the *portrait d'apparat* – posing subjects with objects familiar to them or ones that revealed their trade or station in life, but he was able to make this shopworn technique seem fresh.

His earliest work of note featured his brother and was called *Boy With a Squirrel*. Benjamin West, an American artist living in England, taught many young American artists, and was so impressed that he invited Copley to come to England to study under him. At this point, Copley was not ready to leave his new-found fame behind.

Success enabled Copley to marry, in 1769, a descendant of the first woman to step off the Mayflower onto American soil. They lived in comfort on Beacon Hill while the conflict between Great Britain and the Colonies increased in force and tempo. Torn between loyalties, Copley tried to keep his distance from politics, which he considered to be disadvantageous to both art and artist. But his in-laws were loyal to the crown; his father-in-law was the merchant who had bought the tea that would be dumped into the harbor during the Boston Tea Party.

Copley's attempts to serve as middleman between the opposing forces were to no avail. Fellow artists urged him to leave the country. In 1774 his house was stormed by a mob angry about his socializing with British army officers. That proved the final straw. Copley sailed for England to study with Benjamin West, leaving his wife, mother and children behind. The following year, at his insistence, they joined him abroad. The family never returned to America.

Once in England, Copley turned his hand to making money. As historical art was currently more in vogue than portraiture, he set about painting in a new genre, producing in 1778 one of his most famous works, *Watson and the Shark*, an example of the Romantic period's great theme of man vs. nature.

Copley had discovered a fine way to get the most money out of a single work of art: he painted the picture, exhibited it himself (charging admission), sold reproduction rights, and finally sold the picture itself. The Royal Academy, of which he was now a member, disliked the practice, but were not able to dissuade him from it.

Although most of his work produced abroad never equaled the vitality and realism of his earlier work, he remained popular and busy until his death in 1815, even painting portraits of John Adams and John Quincy Adams while they were visiting England.

Still, this accomplished artist might have grown up to be a seller of tobacco, had chance not "thrown the boy Copley into one of the few households in all the Colonies where art was the predominant interest."

Henry William Carmichael-Smyth, stepfather of

WILLIAM MAKEPEACE THACKERAY,
English novelist, born 1811

"[T]here were times. . . when Thackeray was to exclaim impatiently at 'that stupid old Governor of mine.' But when he put him into a book and called him Colonel Newcome, it was the Major's shining virtue — his intrinsic goodness — that he made to stand out way beyond his frailties. With his courtly code of honour, his kindness and integrity, he provided Thackeray with a model he was long to use as a yardstick for the world." Ann Monsarrat, biographer

The story of how Captain Henry William Carmichael-Smyth came to be the stepfather of William Makepeace Thackeray reads like a wild plot line out of one of the romantic novels of the day: secret trysts, treachery and deception, and eventual fulfillment of the characters' destinies. Carmichael-Smyth was a dedicated young officer of good family but little money, which disqualified him as a suitable suitor for young Anne Becher — at least in the eyes of her grandmother. When their secret meetings in Grandmama's garden were discovered, they managed to continue for a time by letter. Then Grandmama Becher decided to return his letters and to tell her granddaughter that her lover had died of a sudden mysterious illness.

6

Anne was devastated, and as soon as a good excuse was found, she was dispatched to India along with her sister, where everyone was sure a good match could be found for both girls among English society there. The ruse worked in its entirety, and both girls were married within a year. Her sister found a suitable young Army officer, and Anne's husband, Richmond Thackeray, was rising in the ranks of the Foreign Service.

In less than a year, Anne and Richmond became parents of a son, who was large enough to render the birth particularly difficult, and Anne was advised to have no more children.

After a long recovery, Anne was finally able to host a dinner party and resume her social life as usual. Imagine her shock and disbelief when one of the guests was announced as Captain Carmichael-Smyth of the Bengal Engineers. In one of those impossible coincidences that any movie or literary critic would decry as unbelievable, Richmond Thackeray had encountered the Captain at his club and, upon discovering that he was new and still friendless, invited him home to dinner.

Later, the Captain told Anne how her grandmother had explained that Anne no longer had any interest in him—and he believed her. Honor, and the closeness of the British community, dictated that her husband be informed of this new and disconcerting state of affairs. When he was, he "listened gravely, said little, but was never the same to Anne again." Three years later, he died of a fever, leaving his family moderately well off.

Anne married the faithful Henry Carmichael-Smyth, but packed up little five-year-old Billy and sent him to live with relatives in England, where he missed India in general and his mother in particular. He was not to see her again until he was nine years old. The child may have been a living reminder to Anne of his grandmother's duplicity in the loss of her first love, an extremely painful childbirth, or the inability to have a child with Henry. Whatever the reason, thereafter on Billy's birthday, it was always he who wrote to his mother, instead of she to him, to mark the event.

Thackeray started school at a fairly agreeable place, but was soon transferred by his parents to a boarding school, where conditions were so wretched that he complained all his life about having been beaten and starved by the tyrannical headmaster. One good memory stands out from this generally miserable time. On occasion, the headmaster would take some of the boys to the theater, which Thackeray developed into a lifelong taste.

When Captain and Mrs. Carmichael-Smyth returned to England around 1820, they intended it to be only a vacation. Instead, the Captain was promoted to Major and his father died. Henry decided to remain in England. The cost of living was vastly higher there, but now they could more readily afford it.

Despite being reasonably well off, the Carmichael-Smyth family espoused many liberal causes and passed their political taste on to young William. His step-uncle James, while Governor of the Bahamas, was known as an abolitionist and a foe of capital punishment for slaves, championed the rights of female slaves, and was constantly at war with the local legislators as well as landowners.

At this point, Thackeray was sent to Charterhouse school, where all the men of his stepfather's family were educated. Called "the best school of them all," it was full of unruly boys and employed a singularly bad system, whereby newcomers were instructed and supervised by older students. An endless variety of corporal punishments were administered, including bashing an inattentive student in the head with a book. One can only wonder what the schools of lesser repute were like.

The headmaster, Dr. Russell, excelled at the art of verbal abuse, which Thackeray found far more humiliating than any physical punishment. In his early literary works, Thackeray renamed Charterhouse; "Slaughter House" neatly encapsulated his feelings toward the school where he claims to have been "abused into sulkiness and bullied into despair."

On one holiday journey home, Thackeray found himself without sufficient funds to complete the trip without using money he was supposed to be taking home to his parents as a refund on an overpayment. By this time, he was accustomed to punishments out of proportion to the crime, and was in agony at the prospect of reporting the shortage to his parents. The Major's response was simply to wonder why he hadn't used even more of the money to eat adequately on the journey.

Thackeray spent as much time as possible reading the currently popular novels, especially those by Sir Walter Scott and James Fenimore Cooper, and *The Arabian Nights.* He developed something of a talent for illustrating his own works, acting, and writing poetry. He and his cronies also loved the periodicals which thrived in mid-nineteenth century England and dreamed of writing and editing such literary vehicles themselves. As Thackeray advanced in school, he kept a brotherly eye on the younger boys, especially his cousin Charley, the half-Indian son of his uncle Charles Carmichael-Smyth.

At seventeen, Thackeray was removed from school and sent to private tutors. He felt as though he had been released from shackles. The Major had been Governor of the East India Company's military academy but left the post in 1824, just as Thackeray was leaving Charterhouse. Now on an estate in Devon, Thackeray spent a great deal of time simply reading and attending the theater. When the Major decided his stepson had wasted enough time, he began tutoring him in person in preparation for entrance into Cambridge, where he had gone.

Life with his mother had turned difficult. Now in constant contact with her, Thackeray began to temper his childhood adoration with the realization that she was possessive, demanding, and passionate about her attachments, even when they seemed contradictory—she was a social radical yet a religious fundamentalist. It was with a great sense of relief that he set off for Cambridge, with the Major as escort, and settled into his lodgings there.

He never finished his degree. Instead he spent time in Germany soaking up the local culture and procrastinating about his future. A process of elimination left only law as a suitable pursuit. He read law at the Middle Temple in London, but the law proved, in the final analysis, to be of as little interest as anything else. Gambling and other profligacies occupied most of his time, with the result that he ran through nearly all the inheritance left by his father and was faced at last with the prospect of settling into some profession.

With the backing of his grandmother and stepfather, he bought a newspaper, *The National Standard,* becoming its chief contributor as well as editor, illustrator and advertising manager. Despite his efforts, *The Standard* eventually failed.

While in Paris to study art, he met his future wife, Isabella. His parents, convinced of his serious intentions, decided to help him find work lucrative enough to allow him to marry. The Major, who never had minded investing in chancy propositions, tried one more: he helped found a politically radical newspaper called *The Constitutional*, with the intention of naming Thackeray its Paris correspondent. The entire family threw themselves into the chore of drumming up funds from backers and shareholders and selling subscriptions.

Thackeray was indeed named Paris correspondent but drew a good salary only because his stepfather forfeited his own salary as director. At least now Thackeray would be able to marry. By and large, *The Constitutional* was just a façade propped up by Major Carmichael-Smyth, who really couldn't afford to make such a sacrifice. By the time Thackeray and Isabella had produced their first child, *The Constitutional* was bankrupt and the Major had to flee to Paris to avoid creditors. Thackeray was on his own.

Immediately he set about taking any and all writing or drawing commissions that came his way, on one occasion even trading an original poem for a new carpet. What little remained of his inheritance he signed over to the Major, as partial repayment for his generosity, and also perhaps to keep himself from squandering it, as the newlyweds seemed to have a penchant for spending every penny they had.

Thackeray frequented a variety of social clubs and caroused with his bachelor friends, who could spend with abandon without worrying about depriving a family. Thackeray had one daughter already; the second daughter lived for only eight months. Thackeray moved them all to Paris, where he could finish a novel, and expressed to his mother the hope that the next decade would be better to them than the last.

The following year produced yet another daughter, but Isabella never quite recovered from her third and last pregnancy. She slipped into mental illness and was never to be free of it. Thackeray found himself emotionally unable to provide the constant care and watchfulness she required, so she spent the remainder of her life living with friends and only intermittently with her husband. In his travels on the continent, the Major learned of a treatment called hydrosupathy, which involved alternating courses of sweating and being drenched in cold water. To persuade Isabella to participate, both he and Thackeray took the cure along with her. It seemed to work—for a time—but Isabella eventually retreated into violence and suicidal tendencies.

During the 1840s, Thackeray's reputation as a writer grew, and in 1846 he bought a house in London so he could live with his daughters, who had been in the care of his mother. Annie, the elder, was reportedly becoming hard to handle—which, when said of a girl child in Victorian England, might only mean that she was intelligent, imaginative, and a bit cheeky—so the hunt for a governess was on. Thackeray describes his plight as follows: "Unless I liked a Governess, I couldn't live with her and if I did—O fie. The flesh is very weak, *le coeur sent toujours le besoin d'aimer.*" He and Isabella had been unable to live as man and wife for years, and he wisely saw the inappropriateness of having an attractive woman live in his house and care for his children.

The thought of where such temptation might lead him evidently distressed him so much that he had to express it in French—"the heart always has need of love"—or perhaps he was simply being cautious because he was writing to his mother. The last great attachment of his life was Jane Brookfield, the wife of a long-time friend, but this affair, while passionate, was entirely platonic. Still, when her husband insisted that it end, Thackeray was as grief-stricken as he had been at his wife's mental decline and the resulting dissolution, for all practical purposes, of their marriage.

Finding that he needed constant distraction in order not to dwell on his problems, Thackeray spent as much time as he could working or caring for his daughters. He had tried to persuade his parents to come and live with them, but the Major held out for separate residences. Eventually Thackeray realized the wisdom of this, as it would have resulted in a constant tug of war for supremacy with his mother, whose effect on his children was so distressing that he thought of putting a clause in his will to the effect that they should in no circumstances be allowed to live with her.

In 1848 Thackeray's most famous work, *Vanity Fair*, previously serialized, was issued in bound volumes. As his fame as a writer was assured, he took an advance on his next book and paid off all his stepfather's debts. By 1859, he was able to persuade his parents to live in London, where he provided a house for them as well as funds to maintain it. They lived there for two years until the Major's death. Thackeray journeyed to Scotland, where the Major had been visiting ancestral haunts, and buried him in a churchyard in Ayr. On his tombstone were the words from what had become one of the best beloved scenes in English literature, the death of a character, which Thackeray had modeled on Major Carmichael-Smyth: "*Adsum*—And lo, he whose heart was as that of a little child, had answered to his name, and stood in the presence of The Master."

George Leveson-Gower, Earl Granville, stepfather of

LORD ACTON, English historian, b. 1834

"What was important to Leveson — [which] he made available to Acton — was a social and political environment which defined his character, his career and his interests." Gertrude Himmelfarb, biographer

John Emerich Edward Dalberg Acton, known to history as Lord Acton, has been called "the most learned Englishman alive," but may be best known to the world as the source of the much-quoted maxim "Power tends to corrupt and absolute power corrupts absolutely."

This British peer, whose place in history was felt mostly through his influence on those around him, never wrote a book, never earned a degree, and started far more projects than he finished. The premier vehicle for intellectual argument and the dissemination of ideas in Victorian England was the review or magazine, where Acton excelled, and his decades-long friendship with the statesman William Gladstone may have had an untold effect on the politics of the day.

Acton's was a life of contradictions. A devout Catholic, he was always suspicious of arbitrary power, which was sure to put him on a collision course with Rome sooner or later. Also a devout historian, he advocated applying the scientific approach to the study of both history and religion, and was certain that absolute moral judgment could be applied to both fields, a stance which put him at odds with many of his contemporaries, as well as with the modern world of relative judgments. In a sense, Acton stood alone in history, a position of which he himself was keenly aware.

John Acton's mother, Lady Acton, was widowed when her son was three years old, a position to which her actions may have contributed. Her husband, whose carousing and gambling displeased her immensely, returned home drunk late one night only to find the door locked and no one disposed to let him in. He reportedly caught a chill and died of pneumonia.

The family remained living in Paris for a time, so little John grew up speaking French with his mother. By the time he was eight years old, he spoke four languages. In the Paris social scene, Lady Acton met and fell in love with George Leveson-Gower, and they married in 1840 when John was six years old.

Despite her being older than he was, the major objection to the match was religious—he was Anglican, she Catholic—and a tortuous compromise had to be worked out with the Church and both families about how future children would be raised and educated. As it turned out, there were none, but at this time in history, such arrangements were taken very seriously.

There does not seem to have been much of an emotional connection between Johnny, as he was called, and his new stepfather. Their tastes and temperaments were quite dissimilar, which became more obvious as time went by. In his biography *Lord Acton*, Roland Hill states: "Leveson was a worldly man, relaxed about everything in life, whereas his precocious stepson had an anxious as well as a serious religious disposition."

Nor was Johnny happy to be separated so much from his mother, who was expected to do her part on the social scene, as her new husband was advancing in the ranks of the Whig party that currently ruled England. Leveson was not only appointed Undersecretary of State for Foreign Affairs, but soon succeeded his father as Earl [later Lord] Granville.

At age eight, Johnny was given to a tutor to improve his English. Having been raised abroad, he spoke mainly German and French. He was then sent to St. Mary's, Oscott, where he alternated between happiness and despair, and once reported that he excelled at two arts—chess and pick-pocketing. He was becoming quite a linguist; by age ten, he was at ease in at least nine languages.

Even at this young age, he stated an ambition to write an outline of history for his own reference, and to establish "a perfect library," goals which he worked toward as an adult, even if he did not quite achieve both of them. Johnny seemed to be making overtures to his stepfather, but these probably did not denote a real attachment, but rather an attempt to bridge the gap between himself and the person who had abruptly shown up in his life and taken over his mother's time and affection.

Leveson, now called Granville, was evidently not impressed by Johnny's performance at school, and sent him off to study in Edinburgh for two years with a private tutor. Johnny felt exiled. Although this was to be preparation for his entry into Cambridge University, it and two other colleges rejected him on religious grounds. This setback turned into a boon, as much of Acton's future thought was shaped by the next stage of his education.

Relatives in Germany were on good terms with well-known scholar Dr. Ignaz von Döllinger. Acton set about persuading his stepfather to send him there to study with this respected Catholic academic, even if it required some flattery and backpedaling. Granville naturally wanted his stepson to enter politics, but Acton was envisioning a rather different future for himself. More enchanted by the world of pure ideas and scholarship than the political arena, he was eager to go to Germany to study.

Acton liked the Doctor a great deal, although he ascribed Döllinger's achievements "more to his character and industry than to his innate genius." He was greatly impressed by the man's library, which motivated him to establish his own library at his English estate of Aldenham. Granville encouraged this by increasing his allowance for the purpose of buying books.

In his mother's absence, Acton grew quite fond of Countess Arco, his German relative and hostess, and wished to remain in Munich as long as possible. The Granvilles wanted him to return to continue his studies in England, but Dr. Döllinger apparently talked them out of it with enthusiastic reports of young John's progress and achievements. Acton also became friendly with Professor Ernst von Lasaulx, and acquired the professor's library when he died.

By 1854 Acton was back at his inherited English home, Aldenham. His stepfather, who had been overseeing it during his minority, wanted the estate, but Johnny had no desire to lose the independence that owning the place gave him. While remaining polite, he declined the offer. Granville had little confidence in his stepson's ability to run the estate, but had no choice.

Acton's main interest, however, was in increasing and improving his library. Ironically, years later he bequeathed it to Cambridge University, despite its earlier refusal to admit him.

Lord Granville attempted to interest his stepson in foreign service or the political arena by encouraging him to participate in several trips abroad in the early 1850's. A journey to New York to an industrial exhibition yielded some exposure to American democracy via a Massachusetts State Constitutional Convention; Acton was horrified by the generally low level of erudition and decorum, as typified by the fact that one speaker advocated votes for women. A visit to Russia to attend the coronation of Tsar Alexander II was enjoyed far more by Granville than Acton.

As for his stepfather's pushing him toward politics, Acton himself stated clearly, "I am conscious of no political ambition, and I have an aversion and an incapacity for official life," and said as much to his stepfather. Perhaps Granville mistook this for a simple aversion to the current government, but Acton's entire temperament was unsuited to the life. He felt that, for one thing, he was first a Catholic and only secondly a Whig, which would render him incapable of true party loyalty. However, some of his deeply-felt convictions pushed him into conflict with the Church as well.

Initially, however, he acquiesced. In those times, Acton could be and was eventually elected to represent a small borough in Ireland, with which he had absolutely no prior connection. Acton was a reluctant politician and made very little contribution to the business of governance, though by his very first vote, he did help bring a new government into power—one which was to include William Gladstone as Chancellor of the Exchequer.

Although he rather disliked Gladstone early on, their friendship later ripened into one that would provide an intellectual underpinning for a great deal of the politics of Victorian England, especially when Gladstone rose to be Prime Minister. Acton and Gladstone were familiar with each other's work as published in various magazines and journals of the times, including *The Rambler*, a Catholic review which Acton edited and wrote for. Gladstone was more impressed by Acton's views than vice versa.

Acton's first speech in Parliament regarding Italian unification was well received both by that body and by Lord Granville, who sent a copy to Countess Arco and commented mostly on Johnny's deportment and delivery rather than on the content of the speech, which itself may be indicative of the very different temperaments of the two men. Johnny was making a philosophical point, but Granville was pleased because "His future success in the House is certain." Acton himself, while expressing happiness that he had not let his stepfather down, also said, "If I could only get turned out of Parliament in an honest way, and settle down among my books."

At last he was, and at that point told his future wife, "I have never regretted my defeat for one moment. . ." Granville, finally aware of Acton's true feelings, wrote to him, "I cannot tell you how sorry I am (possibly more than you are)."

Acton gave the following account of his aims and intentions in a letter to his wife:

"[T]he one supreme object of all my thoughts is the good of the Church. . .The greatest good that I can do is by means of literature, for there I have resources greater than any other person, and I have collected materials of imminent extent. .

.Political influence, and that of a very valuable kind, I shall always continue to possess while my friendship with Gladstone lasts, and while he is a leading statesman—for in Catholic matters he trusts me more than anybody. . ."

Acton's mother had died before she could see him married to his German cousin Marie Arco-Valley, whom she favored, but Granville, at least in part to honor his wife's memory, tried to further the match despite Marie's hesitation. He counseled his stepson to offer continued friendship in hopes that her feelings would eventually ripen into love, and it seems to have happened exactly that way. They married in 1865 and eventually had six children.

Through *The Rambler* and later *The Home and Foreign Review,* Acton became widely known as a historian and commentator on the political scene, with a bent toward a gradual unfolding of truth and freedom, holding that stability fosters liberty, and that the individual conscience is the true basis of morality, not any outside power.

As a defender of freedom, Acton came down on the wrong side when the Catholic Church instituted the doctrine of Papal Infallibility, and indeed organized the opposition to it. When the final vote was taken in the Church Council, the yeas carried the day. His old friend Döllinger was excommunicated, but Acton relented enough to save himself, avowing that "communion with Rome [is] dearer than life." Later Acton proposed to write a biography of the professor, but it was never finished, although he did produce a laudatory essay on Döllinger's life and work.

In 1869 Acton was elevated to the House of Lords, partly through the influence of Lord Granville and Gladstone, both of whom wished to see him more active in politics, but his major interest in his new position seemed to be the "splendid library. . .which I propose to enjoy greatly." More than once in the next decade or so, John Acton was suggested for important diplomatic posts but nothing materialized. Several times he was proposed for the position of Ambassador to Berlin. With his perfect command of German, Bavarian wife, and countless European connections, he would have been an excellent candidate, but Lord Granville evidently objected. In later years, there was talk of placing Acton in Gladstone's cabinet, but that met with opposition from both political rivals and jealous friends.

In 1890, when Lord Granville died, Acton did not attend the funeral, but confessed to Gladstone that he was ashamed of himself, calling Granville "your best friend and mine." That may have been merely politeness and respect for the dead, as he had deeply offended Granville's second wife by publishing letters revealing himself to have had little regard for her husband's abilities. Granville's career may have been extended in years, but it reflected no great vision or talent for statesmanship. Acton dismissed him as having little knowledge of foreign countries, religion, or human nature, and little liking for foreigners, which leads one to wonder how, if true, he could have been even barely functional as Foreign Secretary. The disdain was mutual, and in an 1870 letter to Gladstone, Granville proclaimed his stepson a failure in all his public endeavors.

Acton continued to submit to the journals and newspapers, gave lectures, and received a number of honorary degrees before being appointed Professor of Modern History at Cambridge, the university which had earlier rejected him as a student. He helped found the *English Historical Review,* and was in the middle of amassing a huge project called *The Cambridge Modern History* when he died in 1902.

Contact with his stepfather had been random after his mother's death and problematic even before, and yet, without Granville's prodding of his reluctant stepson, and insistence upon the proper education, Acton might have remained nothing more than an English country squire who amassed a 70,000 volume library and lived quietly amidst his beloved books. He would undoubtedly have published, but the secondary effects of his entrance into public life would never have been felt. As Matthew Arnold once noted, "Gladstone influences all around him but Acton; it is Acton who influences Gladstone."

Washington Ferguson, stepfather of

BOOKER T. WASHINGTON, educator, lecturer, b. 1856

"My stepfather had already secured job at a salt-furnace,
and he had also secured a little cabin for us to live in."

Booker T. Washington was born into slavery on the
Burrough's farm near Hale's Ford, Virginia. His mother was a
cook. No one is quite sure who his father was, but Booker's
gray eyes and reddish hair led everyone to suspect he must
have been a white man, possibly a son of the neighboring farmer,
who owned Booker's future stepfather. Such things were far
from uncommon in those days, and Booker did not seem to be
very curious about it.

"Whoever he was," said Booker, "I never heard of his taking
the least interest in me or providing in any way for my rearing."
He was quick to add that he was in no way bitter about this, nor
did he find any particular fault with the man, who was "simply
another unfortunate victim" of the social and political conditions
fo the time. This accepting, conciliatory attitude lasted a lifetime,
and was to bring him into conflict with more radical black
leaders.

Booker's stepfather, Washington Ferguson, infrequently visited the Burroughs plantation. His owner, Josiah Ferguson, was known to be a cruel man. Many of his slaves, perhaps understandably enough, were considered to be troublemakers, "Wash" among them, so he was allowed to work off the plantation to avoid dealing with him. Wash seemed to enjoy the relative freedom and variety, even if his wages did go directly to his master, and told tales about his various experiences that fascinated young Booker, who had never been off the plantation. Wash was already in his 50's, but he wasn't too old to make good his escape during the Civil War.

Many freed slaves, especially of the older generation, had no idea what to do with themselves after emancipation and so contracted with former owners for the services they had provided before. It seemed that Booker's mother, Jane, would do the same thing. Then Wash sent a wagon for Jane and her three children—Amanda, her daughter with Ferguson, and her two older sons. Jane, who had asthma and heart trouble, rode on the wagon with what possessions they had, while the children made the 200 mile trip to West Virginia mostly on foot.

Lack of sanitation, boredom, and unbelievably hard work made for horrible conditions at the salt mines in Malden, West Virginia, where Wash worked, but somehow the family survived. Wash soon put Booker and his older brother John to work packing salt just like he did; it was exhausting work and the hours were sometimes from before dawn until dark. The boys hated the work and resented the fact that Wash pocketed their earnings, but such arrangements were the norm, especially among the poorest of the poor where every penny counted.

Booker's sole ambition was to do something not a single black person of his acquaintance could do: read and write. Somehow he persuaded his mother to get him a spelling book, from which he laboriously taught himself the alphabet. About this time a young man showed up looking for the family that his father, an escaped slave, had left behind years ago. He had little success at that, but stayed and set up a school for locals of all ages. Booker yearned to further his education, but Wash was against it—the boy's financial contribution was too desperately needed. At first, Booker could only wangle after-school lessons from the teacher. Finally, he convinced his stepfather to let him work part time and go to school. It was worth it to him to get up before dawn and work until nine, then go to school, and return to work after school.

Booker encountered one unexpected difficulty in school: most of the children had surnames, whereas he had simply been called Booker for as long as he could remember. By his own account, when the teacher called his name, he simply answered "Booker Washington." He did not elaborate on the reasons for his choice.

Some have speculated that he must have meant to honor President George Washington. It is more likely that this uneducated child simply chose a name closer to his own life and experience—that of his stepfather. Why he chose his first name rather than his last name is a mystery. Later, he learned that his mother had named him "Booker Taliaferro," so he incorporated that into his name as well.

When Booker was older, he became the houseboy for Mrs. Ruffner,* whose husband owned the local mines. He was evidently treated quite well in her household and she was remembered by him for encouraging his education.

In 1872, at sixteen, Booker's parents allowed him to go to Hampton Institute, a school for blacks in Virginia. He worked his way through school as a janitor. Two years later, his beloved mother died while he was on his way home for a visit. Booker was devastated and nearly didn't return to school.

Wash Ferguson evidently went through a period of disorientation after the death of his wife. It would be unmanly for him to do household chores, but he was financially unable to hire help. He depended too much upon his teenaged daughter Amanda. A disabling accident eventually led to his leaving the mines, but he stayed in the area, later serving as deacon of a local Baptist Church and working as a janitor.

Booker did return to Hampton, graduated in 1876, and taught in a rural school for three years. Hampton had emphasized vocational training and Booker found he had to start with the basics as well. There was a lot to be taught aside from reading and writing; some of his students had never even heard of a toothbrush.

He began studies at Wayland Seminary, but became disillusioned with the typical classical education as being totally unrelated to what newly freed American blacks really needed. Practical manual training seemed more germane to him.

Booker taught for a time at Hampton Institute and in 1881 was invited to head the new college in Tuskegee, Alabama. Opposition by local white neighbors abated when they learned that these students would be learning practical skills, which included building a kiln and producing the bricks to build their own buildings. Tuskegee Institute became a force in educating local black farmers about better agricultural methods. In 1900 Booker founded the National Negro Business League to encourage blacks to start their own businesses. He toured the country on fund-raising expeditions and became well known to blacks and whites alike as a speaker and advocate for black education.

In 1895 he was asked to speak at the Cotton States Exposition, unheard of for a black man, and delivered a speech that became known as The Atlantic Compromise. He proposed that blacks would be better served by concentrating on economic rather than political freedom, by accepting segregation and simply trying to better themselves personally and professionally by working within the system. White America cheered; black leaders denounced him as The Great Accommodator, and never forgave him. Organizations such as The National Association for the Advancement of Colored People sprang up in opposition.

Booker T. Washington was now seen by the white establishment as the leading black spokesman in America, even meeting with President Theodore Roosevelt to discuss political appointments, another unprecedented event. There was talk of elevating him to a cabinet post, but he quickly discouraged that, preferring to work from outside the system. He was given an honorary degree by Harvard in the 1890's and died in 1915. His birthplace is now a national monument.

Booker kept track of his stepfather through the years but in a somewhat perfunctory, dutiful manner. Wash and Amanda were, after all, his last ties with his mother, whom he had adored. When Wash died in 1896, his sister Amanda's telegrams to her brother show an odd confusion in terminology: "Uncle Wash is barely alive," followed by, "We think Furgeson [sic] is dying," and a week later "Father is dead."

Slaves had usually been referred to by only given names or by given names and their masters' surnames. Upon emancipation, many kept those names, many chose names connected with freedom. For some reason, Booker T. Washington chose to rename himself, not as a Ferguson or a Burroughs, names that could have referred to his former masters, but as a Washington, a name that, to him, may have meant the only father he had ever known.

* *Ruffner descendants located two of Booker's granddaughters and invited them to their family reunion in 1999. Edith (Washington) Johnson and her sister Margaret (Washington) Clifford accepted.*

Lorenzo Scatena, stepfather of

A.P. GIANNINI, banker, b. 1870

"My father broke down at ["Pop's"] funeral. It was the first time in my life
I had ever seen him cry." Giannini's daughter

Try to imagine a world without individual checking accounts, credit cards, installment loans, or branch banks on every corner; a world where hiding your life savings under the mattress was not an eccentricity but simply the norm. Unbelievable?

This was the way the world operated one hundred years ago, before Amadeo Peter Giannini almost single-handedly revolutionized the world of banking.

Born in San Jose, California, A.P., as he was known, was the son of Italian immigrants Luigi and Virginia Giannini, who came to America in 1869. Luigi first ran a hotel which catered mostly to other immigrants, then bought a farm and successfully raised and sold fruits and vegetables for the next two years. Accounts vary somewhat, but in 1876, Luigi was killed over a grievance concerning a few dollars supposedly owed to the man who shot him. In one version of the story, he died in the arms of his seven-year-old son.

The family survived the initial shock due to the efforts of Virginia Giannini, who was, by all accounts, a remarkable woman. Although pregnant with her third son at the time of her husband's death, she managed to carry on with the business and was thought of as an excellent businesswoman.

Still, it must have been difficult to manage the farm and raise three young children by herself. In 1877 she married Lorenzo Scatena, a teamster [wagon driver], who had sometimes helped out by giving her a ride into the city. Scatena was fond of his stepchildren—A.P., "Doc," and George—and they called him "Pop" for the rest of his life, as did many of his close friends.

Scatena was an honest man and a hard worker, but was not particularly ambitious—until he met Virginia Giannini, who had enough ambition for both of them. She had been the driving force behind her first husband's immigration to America.

Nnow she began prodding Lorenzo to move into the city, where he could go into the commission business and her children could attend city schools and get the best education possible. They moved to San Jose in 1879, and later to San Francisco, where Pop took a job with a large commission firm.

As a middleman, he was responsible for selling each farmer's entire stock of produce in one day—or anything unsold of these perishables became a total loss. Scatena became so adept at moving produce that his wife was sure he deserved a raise. When he asked and was refused, Virginia advised him to quit and start his own business. Soon, L. Scatena and Company was as successful a business as anyone could want, and the family moved to a better location.

A.P. was a serious, almost driven, student, who did very well in school, despite the fact that he frequently slipped out of the house at night and followed his stepfather to work. Scatena obligingly explained the business to A.P., who was plainly fascinated and absorbed every detail. The young man began a lively advertising campaign to solicit business for his stepfather's company, sending letters to growers all over the area. Orders came in from all quarters, to the unsuspecting Scatena's surprise. Finally his bookkeeper told him that his son had been working on this project for quite a while. A. P. also came up with the perceptive notion of copying boats' manifests, so they would know exactly what merchandise was to be available on any given day, thus giving them an advantage over less well-informed competitors.

A.P. knew his mother would not approve of his moonlighting, so he sneaked out of the house carrying his shoes. The world of business began to absorb all of his time and thought. There was no way school could compete with the real world of commerce, and eventually he simply stopped going to school. His mother naturally objected, and at her insistence, he attended business school for a short time.

At fifteen, A. P. was already full grown and had a man's ability to work, compete, and survive in the rough and tumble atmosphere of the docks.

"I don't think he ever lost an account or a contest of any kind," one rival merchant said. "No one could bluff, intimidate, or out-general him."

His legendary self-confidence plus his growing reputation for personal integrity made him the best salesman in the area. Described as "impatient. . .high-strung and crazy with ideas. . .," A.P. was soon made chief buyer for the entire region by his proud, and practical, stepfather.

At age nineteen, he was made a full partner in the firm. Ordinarily that meant buying one's way in, but Pop knew his boy, and arranged to be paid out of the future profits he had no doubt would materialize. And they did.

By the time A.P. retired from the business in 1901, most of his competitors had either gone out of business or were working for him. The challenge was gone—it was time to move on. The object had never been money. "I don't ever want to be rich," A.P. had been known to say. "No man actually ever owns a fortune—it owns him."

During this time, A.P. fell in love and decided to marry. Not minding in the least that his intended wife was already engaged, he started a nonstop courtship, with Pop's blessing. "I'll never want another and nobody else is going to have her," A.P. averred, to which his stepfather replied, "Go get her, my boy." The outcome was never in doubt. Clorinda Cuneo and A. P. married in 1897.

Although A.P. and Scatena also entered into the real estate business together and couldn't seem to lose money if they tried, that wasn't to be the final focus of their lives. A. P.'s most significant achievements in business were to be in another field entirely—and he was now only thirty-one years old.

Upon the death of his father-in-law, Giannini was asked to manage the Cuneo family's vast holdings, including the Columbus Savings and Loan Society. The bank's Board of Directors welcomed Giannini (and his reputation) to the Board. He insisted they also elect Scatena as a Director. They Board soon regretted it. True to form, Giannini began proposing wild, avant garde ideas such as actually lending to small businesses and hard-working individuals rather than just to large firms and the wealthy.

The majority of the Board voted against him, going so far as to fire Scatena from the Board while he was absent, on vacation in Italy. If Giannini was unhappy about that, imagine his response when he discovered that some of the Board members were involved in various illegal practices to fatten their own fortunes. Furious at both their shortsightedness and their underhandedness, Giannini stormed out—and promptly created his own bank where he could implement his own ideas without opposition.

The Bank of Italy, started up with $150,000 contributed by Scatena and several of his friends, worked out of a converted saloon right across the street from Columbia Savings and Loan. Almost as a final insult to his elitist rivals, he hired the former bartender as a teller. The only condition attached to the money Scatena put up was that consideration for loans would be given to rich and poor alike, with no distinction, other than, one supposes, a reasonable expectation that the loan would be repaid.

Giannini readily agreed, adding that his bank would be run "solely for the benefit of the stockholders and depositors. . .No man will be permitted to win power enough to dominate its policies unwisely. No officer, including myself, shall be tied up with outside interests."

As he had earlier in the produce commission business, Giannini eagerly sought business, soliciting anyone he thought a likely customer. Iit was still necessary to explain to the man on the street what a bank actually did, since most banks did not care to deal with small accounts. Until the bank was on its feet, Giannini and Scatena worked without salary, but in eight months they were paying dividends, and a year later the Bank of Italy had over a million dollars in assets.

Then came the San Francisco earthquake of 1906. Giannini managed to salvage two million dollars in gold and securities, which he transported by wagon, hidden beneath a load of vegetables, to a safer location. The next day, against the advice of more cautious lenders, he was making dockside loans from an office consisting of a plank over two barrels, asking only for a signature to guarantee the money necessary to help rebuild a business or a life. In years to come, he lent money in areas disdained by the more conservative banking establishment; as a result, California was able to develop its fledgling wine and motion picture industries, as well as many agricultural ventures.

Giannini studied the flaws in the banking system and thought he saw at least a partial solution. The system of branch banking—locally managed offices under one Board of Directors and able to access the capital of the whole—was not a totally new idea, although it had never been made to work in the United States. By 1909 he was buying up banks all over California, and twenty years later the Bank of Italy became the Bank of America.

Giannini "retired" again in 1930 and passed leadership of the bank to others. This turned out to be an ill-conceived move, as his hand-picked successor began selling off branches and dismissing bank officers loyal to Giannini. Having personally propped up the bank's stock during the crash of 1929, Giannini felt betrayed. He came back from Europe, where he had been living, to try to reconstitute the company as he had envisioned it. He had always urged employees and depositors to own shares in "their" bank, and so he mounted a campaign to get their proxies in an attempt to regain control. He succeeded, with 63% of the stockholders behind him.

In 1930, Lorenzo Scatena had taken ill with uremic poisoning and was not expected to live. Giannini made exceptional speed on his frantic journey from Europe to California, but arrived three hours too late — Pop had gone into a coma and died.

The eulogy recognized him as a man "of great energy and ambition, but whose greatest success was as a father, who took into his love the three sons of the widow he married." Scatena's passing was one of the few things in his life that would bring Giannini to tears. They had worked side by side through decades of struggle and had created more than one empire together.

By 1947 the Bank of America was the largest bank in the United States. Giannini finally retired for good in 1945, just as the Bank of America was set to finance most of California's post-war economic boom.

Giannini declined all honorary degrees and awards offered him, but served on the Board of Regents of the University of California, where he also established the Foundation of Agricultural Economics, as well as setting up a foundation for medical research and educational scholarships.

When he died, at age seventy-nine, his estate was worth less than $500,000. He had worked for very little pay, and once donated a multi-million-dollar bonus to the University of California.

"Money itch is a bad thing," he is quoted as saying. "I never had that trouble." What he did have trouble with was people who were afraid of change, who were dishonest or lazy, and who had no vision. Between his mother and stepfather, he had been taught to value hard work, ambition, honesty, and creativity. He used those gifts to change the face of the banking industry forever.

Charles B. Shepperson, stepfather of

WILLIAM GRANT STILL, African-American
composer, b. 1895

"He initiated and fostered in me a love for the stage which has never died."

William Grant Still, who grew up to be called "the dean of Negro American composers," was born in Mississippi. His parents, William Grant Sr. and Carrie Lena Fambro Still, had met at Alabama A&M University, where they were both studying to be teachers. William, Sr. died when "Billy" was only three months old; some said he'd been poisoned by person or persons unknown. Such incidents were not unknown in those days. According to another family story, a friend of the elder Still had been run out of Mississippi by local whites, angry that he had become a property owner and "too big for his britches." But somehow, W.G. Still, Sr., who had been a music teacher at Alabama A&M, died before his time, passing only his musical heritage to the son he would never know.

Carrie's mother and sister lived in Little Rock, Arkansas, so the young widow and her infant son went to live there. She took a teaching job at Capital Hill School for African-Americans and taught there until her death in 1927. Among her pupils was her son Billy, who was certainly accorded no favors by his mother, who expected him to excel at everything. For the most part, he did, graduating at sixteen as class valedictorian.

Early influences were his talented and disciplined mother; his grandmother, who loved to sing hymns and spirituals while doing her housework; and the man his mother married in 1904. Charles B. Shepperson was a railway postal clerk with a great love of music, which may have drawn the adults together.

Shepperson was thought of as a dignified man, but he was not too dignified to know how to have fun with a young son. He grinned as he refused to tell Billy what his middle initial stood for. He was happy to share his appreciation of various forms of music with his stepson. Not only did they attend concerts and plays and listen to Shepperson's collection of classical records, they also went on hunting and fishing expeditions and attended the circus. What Billy truly enjoyed was the theater, musical shows, and opera.

He also encouraged Billy's imagination by telling colorful tales of what would otherwise have been a rather prosaic occupation. Shepperson had been a mail clerk on a train which was held up by the infamous Cherokee Bill, and saved himself from bullets by hiding behind piles of mail bags. Once he took Billy to the public trial of a horse thief. To a boy who had loved to read Wild West stories—until Mother removed the temptation as too frivolous for a serious student—these stories and excursions were a wonderful diversion, even better than The Wizard of Oz or Robin Hood onstage.

On a more serious note, Charles B. gave young William a copy of *Plutarch's Lives*. In the copy of *Quo Vadis* that he gave him, he had written: "You must read this. I'm sure you will derive much good from this. The very book for you."

Billy was also exposed to the music of black culture in Little Rock when he accompanied his mother to the many social functions she, as a teacher, was expected to attend. Often folks gathered in the church, before going on to some musical or stage production, and joyously sang lively hymns and spirituals. He accepted this as just one more musical show and, to his mother's chagrin, sometimes clapped for the ladies as though they were performers. His mother also organized dramatic presentations of Shakespearean plays to raise badly needed funds for the school library. There was no lack of theatrical and musical inspiration in Billy's early life.

The first musical instrument he ever learned to play was a toy fiddle he made himself. Noting this early interest, his mother chose the violin as his first instrument for formal training. No sooner had Billy learned to read music than he tried writing his own, making his own manuscript paper by hand, painstakingly drawing in the lines for the musical staff.

After graduation, he went to Ohio to attend Wilberforce University, the oldest private African-American university in the United States. His mother insisted that he study medicine, although his heart was elsewhere. He pursued a career in music while making respectable grades in his college classes: he organized a string quartet in which he played violin; learned oboe, clarinet, piccolo and saxophone; became a member of the college band; and experimented with orchestrating music for the band, which was made easier because of his knowledge of so many different instruments. The one he never took up was piano, which some think actually helped his style as an arranger. It was at Wilberforce that some of his first compositions—songs and band numbers—were played publicly, but this fueled the fires and propelled him out of college and into the world of "real" music.

The real world wasn't particularly kind to Still in those early days, and he ran the gamut of experiences. He played oboe, cello and violin in various orchestras, wearing one of his stepfather's cast-off and altered suits (all he could afford at the time); promised to play the banjo just to get work, even though he had never touched one before in his life; worked in a pool hall; served in the Navy; and suffered through an unhappy young marriage.

Things looked up when he began working with W.C. Handy, "the father of the Blues," as both a touring musician and arranger. Many years earlier, Shepperson had encountered Handy in one of the "black only" railroad cars to which they were both restricted, and Shepperson told him about his musical stepson. Handy recognized the name William Grant Still—he had succeeded Still, Sr. at Alabama A. & M. as a teacher of music. Later, Handy gave the boy a boost into the world of music.

Using the last of a small legacy from his birth father, and a scholarship that had been established especially for him, Still studied violin and music theory at Oberlin College in Ohio.

In 1921 Still played oboe in the New York run of the popular black revue *Shuffle Along*, and wrote music for the orchestra to play "just for fun" when they tired of playing the same songs every night during the popular show's run. According to Still's daughter, Judith, George Gershwin attended a performance and "borrowed" one of these tunes, which became the popular standard "I Got Rhythm."

During his New York stay, Still developed the notion that God had chosen him to serve his race—or better yet, all mankind—by using music to bring people together. He had seen lynchings while traveling the country with Handy and knew that there was a lot to be done. Still had grown up in a more or less racially relaxed area and, like his parents, had friends of both races. Nevertheless, he had witnessed instances of intolerance and outright violence as a boy, and while his parents tried to shield him from overt racism, it simply was not possible.

It is interesting to note that even an article about Little Rock, which appeared in *Colored American Magazine* in 1905, despite its obviously conciliatory tone—"There is no friction of any kind between the two races"—goes out of its way to point out that the "sanitary condition" of the many homes owned by "the Negroes" is quite good, and that all domestic work done for local whites is done by blacks, as well as all public work (garbage, street cleaning and the like).

On Still's first trip to St. Louis, which did not have public segregation, he was astonished to find himself in a washroom that had no signs to tell him whether it was for colored or white. Against this background, Still's achievements stand out with even more clarity.

His earnings from *Shuffle Along* left Still with enough money to apply to the New England Conservatory of Music, where he was told that Mr. George Chadwick, who "acquainted [him] with serious American music," would gladly teach him for nothing. Four months later, Still became recording director of the Black Swan Phonograph Company, and then applied for a scholarship with the French ultramodern composer Edgar Varese. This association actually took him down a fruitless path, as their styles were inherently different. Still soon chose to return to work more congenial to his basic nature. He was so much in demand as an arranger that he could have taken that up as his permanent career, but despite working for such luminaries as Artie Shaw, Sophie Tucker and Paul Whiteman, he felt driven to compose his own music.

"I made an effort to elevate the folk idiom into symphonic form," he said, "though rarely making use of actual folk themes. For the most part, I was developing my own themes in the style of the folk. . .I wrote as I chose, using whatever idiom seemed appropriate to the subject at hand." Still's own background contained racial strains of Negro, Scotch, American Indian, Spanish and Irish, and later experiences brought him into contact with Creole and Hebrew music. He felt free to assimilate anything in his experience and/or ancestry into his music.

In the 1920's, he worked mainly on operas (*Blue Steel, A Bayou Legend*) and ballets (*La Guiablesse, Sahdji*).

In 1931, his *Afro-American Symphony* was "the first major piece of music written by a Negro to be played before an American audience." His daughter said, "He was the original crossover artist. And the crowds loved it."

He was also the first black man to conduct an "important" orchestra—the Los Angeles Philharmonic, playing his own compositions. In 1955 he was the first black to conduct an all-white orchestra in the Deep South.

Countless awards and honorary degrees followed, but although his work was well received in both America and Europe, he had trouble getting it performed, and when it was, it sometimes fell victim to critical abuse. His ballet *Troubled Island*, based upon the life of Haitian liberator, Dessalines, with libretto by Langston Hughes, was panned by critics, despite audience approval, simply because they felt that a black man was on the verge of going too far with his successful career.

34

But other sources tend to emphasize the positive, stating that the work received enthusiastic ovations at its initial performances, which contributed to the New York City Center sponsoring operas written by Americans. His ballet *Sahdji* had the same effect at the American Music Festival in Rochester, NY. Still was frequently to be the one who broke the barrier, paving the way for others.

Nevertheless, the seemingly cool reception of *Troubled Island* cast a shadow over the rest of Still's work, and although he continued to write classical music, much of it was never performed. During this period, Still worked as an arranger and conductor for many popular radio shows, later branching out into TV and movie work.

In 1934 Still moved to California, where he met Verna Arvey, the child of Russian Jewish emigrants. Verna worked as both a journalist and a pianist. She frequently performed works by American black composers, and naturally fell into collaboration with Still, even revising Langston Hughes' libretto for *Troubled Island*. By 1939 they had decided to marry, but were obliged to do so in Mexico, because interracial marriages were still illegal in the United States. They enjoyed a lifelong partnership, during which Still dismissed his former librettist to work solely with his wife.

Still's parents did not live to see most of his best work. Shepperson drowned in 1922, and Carrie succumbed to cancer in 1927, after only a few of Still's first major works were starting to be recognized. His mother had come to understand that her son would never be a doctor, but instead had found fulfillment, and distinction, in writing music. As she had always wanted, he had "made something of himself," and she was pleased with what he had made.

Still's raw talent, received from his parents and encouraged by his music-loving stepfather, had blossomed into a full-blown musical genius. Still himself lived until 1978, by which time he had composed over 200 works in all musical genres—operas, ballets and symphonies included, and his family is still seeking wider recognition and performance of his works.

Theodor Homburger, stepfather of

ERIK H. ERIKSON, psychoanalyst, 1902

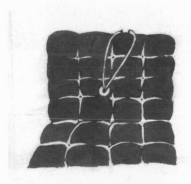

"[M]y stepfather the pediatrician provided me, even in my rebellion, with a daily firm model of identification, centered in the concern for children and in a general Hippocratic orientation."

Called "the most influential living psychoanalyst in America today," and "the closest thing to an intellectual hero in American culture today," Erik H. Erikson was born Erik Salomonsen in Copenhagen, the child of a Jewish mother and an unknown father.

The Abrahamsen family was a strange mixture of traditions, an upper middle class Danish merchant family who spoke no Yiddish and yet maintained many Jewish practices and thought of themselves as Jewish. Karla Abrahamsen was beautiful and brilliant and had an impulsive, artistic temperament which worried her doting father and brother. Her marriage to stockbroker Valdemar Salomonsen hardly lasted until the ink was dry on the marriage license, and no one seems quite sure of the circumstances of its breakdown, other than that she contacted her brother while still on her honeymoon, asking him to come and bring her home. Although Valdemar left the country and Erik was not born until four years later, he is listed as the legal father on the child's birth certificate. Thus was forged the first link in the chain of identity—or lack thereof—that was to form the basis of a life's work for the man who has been called "the architect of identity."

For the first three years of his life, Erik had his mother all to himself and reveled in their special closeness. Then, while traveling through the German city of Karlsruhe, Erik took ill and was taken to a local pediatrician, Dr. Theodor Homburger. The doctor offered not only a solution to a sick child's immediate problem, but also a way out of the somewhat awkward situation of Karla's having given birth to an child that was only technically legitimate. They married on Erik's birthday—and took him with them on their honeymoon.

The Abrahamsens were delighted with Dr. Homburger; Erik was not. To them, he was a prominent Jewish professional man who removed any doubts as to Karla's right to move in respectable society; to Erik, he was an interloper. Oddly enough, they decided to tell Erik that Homburger was his true father, and this "loving deceit" was kept up for quite some time. It is uncertain how they expected this obvious untruth to be maintained, and as a result, from earliest childhood, Erik felt nagging doubts as to his true identity. There was ambivalence on all sides, and for some reason, Erik was not legally adopted for several years.

The Homburgers had two more children, and Theodor's relationship to his daughters was as close as that with his stepson was strained.

Erik watched his mother attempt to maintain a German household, where only German was spoken, while still cultivating her own ties to the Danish culture of her youth by reading Danish newspapers and the works of outstanding Danish Christian philosophers such as Kierkegaard. Karla followed many Jewish customs in the home. As if that didn't produce enough cultural diversification, Erik was physically different from the other children: tall, blond and blue-eyed amidst predominantly short and dark playmates. At school, this earned him the nickname of "goy." Erik tried to out-German the Germans, assuming a super-patriotic political stance.

His stepfather wanted him to become a doctor, but Erik was only interested in art, which may have been simply because he was convinced that his biological father had been a Danish aristocrat with artistic leanings. Repeated attempts to draw the truth from his mother about his father yielded inconsistent information, and that eventually eroded their earlier closeness.

Unable to find a firm direction, Erik traveled and studied art in various locations, notably with Gustav Wolf, who had firm ideas about the relationship between art and essence: "whoever throws out decoration and elaborateness finds the spirit. . .The engraving knife gets rid of all that is insignificant— gets down to that which is essential and basic in the subject. . ." Erik was being drawn to studies that would define identity and essence, ideas which formed the core of his later mature work as a psychoanalyst. But to his stepfather, at this point he was simply a failure.

A friend put him in contact with Anna Freud, who was looking for a tutor for the children of one of her clients. Although Erik had no formal training, she found him to be exactly what she was looking for, and was "impressed by how quickly Erik had bonded with the children and sensed a creative spark as she walked with him." The bond extended to her father, Sigmund Freud, although Erik suspected that he saw in Freud a combination of the qualities of his stepfather and his imagined birth father.

This was the turning point of his life. He was "on his way to becoming Erik Erikson, identity's architect." From there on, his career combined Freud's vision and analysis with Homburger's pediatric calling. His most famous work, *Childhood and Society*, examined the notion that identity is continually forged and reforged throughout one's life, in a continuing attempt to reaffirm one's own basic notion of a self that is independent of any of the labels of culture and society.

In 1930 Erikson took the step that would bring him full circle with his stepfather: he married. In fact, he had three ceremonies with the same woman: one Anglican, one civil, and one Jewish.

His wife Joan, an Episcopalian, ostensibly converted to Judaism in order to satisfy convention, but raised their children as Christians. Although he could not have been called a strict Jew by any standards, Erikson had put off marriage, fearing his parents' reaction to his union with a non-Jew. He was eventually persuaded that it would be even worse to abandon his then-pregnant fiancée, much as his own father had done. After repeated attempts to conceal the news from his stepfather, Erikson was finally obliged to introduce him to his daughter-in-law. To his surprise, Homburger approved of this attractive and strong-willed woman, and she proved to be a bridge between the two of them. They even named their first son Kai Theodor.

With the advent of Nazism, Erikson emigrated to America and tried to persuade Theodor and Karla and their children to come with them, but to no avail. As Jews were prohibited from caring for Gentile patients, Theodor's practice diminished considerably, as did his income. Depressed and suicidal, he was shanghaied to Israel by his daughter, who had talked Karla into bringing him to Italy for a supposed vacation. They lived with their daughter Ellen in Haifa until Theodor's death in 1944, receiving financial support from Erikson the entire time. "Only much later, after his migration to America and after his identity with a rebellious young Karla [mother] had been attenuated, was Erik able to revise his portrayal of Theodor." Homburger's will reflected the extent of their reconciliation, and Erikson was granted equal recognition with the two daughters of his marriage with Karla Abrahamsen.

Much has been made of the fact that Erik Erikson renamed himself upon emigrating to America, but that was, in fact, quite common among refugees during that period, especially those of Jewish heritage. Some have denigrated his choice of the name Erikson—the suffix "son" meaning simply "son of"—which meant that he was "his own father, in the most literal sense a self-made man," or put another way, "the man who invented himself."

The implication was that Erikson was repudiating his Jewishness, but the Eriksons recall it differently. Having been given an annoying nickname in school, Erikson understood that his children resented being called "Hamburger" by Americans unused to European names, and the name Erikson, as applied to the children, stated in no uncertain terms that the boys were "Erik's sons." They would never have to wonder, as he had, who their father might be. And then, there was the final ruling authority: his wife Joan. First "we decided," and then "Joan decided." And that was that.

Nevertheless, the name under which he sought naturalization was "Erik Homburger Erikson" and the name under which he wrote was "Erik H. Erikson." Between Erik the boy and Erikson the man stood Theodor Homburger. After years of flailing, searching and longing, the man in whose footsteps Erik Salomonsen had finally followed was not the vague, shadowy, unknowable father of his childhood imagination, but, with only a few differences, the pediatrician from Karlsruhe, Theodor Homburger.

Will Moore, stepfather of

JOHN LEE HOOKER, blues guitar player, b. 1913

"He is my roots. . .he is the man who caused me [to be] who I am today."

It's hard to imagine someone not knowing how old he is or how many brothers and sisters he had, but John Lee Hooker evidently didn't, and there were no official records to tell him. He knew he was born on a farm outside of Clarksdale, Mississippi, somewhere between 1915 and 1923 (according to the 1920 census, it was 1913). Record keeping was informal and depended largely upon family Bibles and individual memories. There may have been 10 or 13 children in the family, depending upon whether or not you counted only live births. Clarksdale's main claims to fame were that Bessie Smith died there, Ike Turner was born there, and John Lee Hooker claimed it as his hometown--the tiny town of his birth not being on any map.

Reverend William Hooker and his wife Minnie lived on a fair sized farm in the Mississippi Delta, and were hardly poor by local standards. The Hooker family lived by rules and values we hardly find comprehensible today—black didn't mingle with white, parents were addressed as "sir" and "ma'am," and wanting to play blues guitar meant your soul was in serious trouble.

Anecdotally, Hooker's first "instrument" was an inner tube nailed up on a barn door, on which he practiced making whatever sounds he could coax out of such a makeshift contraption. He was given his first guitar by a local musician, who gave him some rudimentary instruction and encouraged an interest that Reverend Hooker found downright sinful. Guitar playing might not be quite in the same category as mass murder, but it was certainly suspect and did not belong in a Christian household — at least not if your ambition was something other than playing for the church choir.

The Hookers divorced when John Lee was in his early teens, and before long, his mother was remarried to a sharecropper named Will Moore. John Lee had little idea what transpired between his parents, but knew they had frequent arguments. John Lee admits to no particular problems with his father other than their disagreement over music. To the elder Hooker, it lead to the death of your soul; to John Lee, it was the very core of his life. If he couldn't make music freely and openly, he'd have to find a new home. Minnie and Will Moore offered him one.

Will was, from all accounts, a fine musician, but not by profession. He was a farmer, originally from Shreveport, Louisiana, who served as sideman for many performers who came to the Clarksdale area. Although he had a good reputation at the local level, he never recorded his music. His only legacy is the sound adopted by John Lee, who claimed to play in an identical style. The relationship between a master craftsman and apprentice, in the world of blues, was frequently as close as that of father and son, so this arrangement was only unique in that Moore actually *was* John Lee's (second) father.

There were plenty of opportunities to have learned from all the traveling musicians who frequented the area, but Will Moore thought John Lee was too young for the rowdy Delta parties he provided entertainment for. So John learned his style from his stepfather.

"I wanted to play just like him," he said. "All I listened to was my stepdaddy, 'cause I was into him just like he was God."

Moore gave the boy a new guitar and taught him sounds that he had heard from others but stamped with his own style. John Lee learned that originality might or might not mean that you actually "wrote" a song. What you did was stamp yourself on whatever you played, so that any sound you produced seemed to be uniquely your own.

Will Moore's sound was the boogie. John Lee attributes his first major hit song, *Boogie Chillen*, directly to Moore. "I got that from my stepdad. That was his tune. That was his beat."

John Lee knew he had no future in music if he stayed where he was, so around 1933 he set off for Memphis, the closest destination a kid with basically no money could reach. Racially, morally and musically, Memphis was looser than Clarksdale. John Lee was making the enormous salary of $2-3/week for ushering in a black movie theater while living with an aunt who owned a boarding house. His family found him after a couple of weeks and came after him, but he was determined and left again, eventually winding up in Detroit by way of Cincinnati. He held a number of menial jobs along the way and began playing guitar at parties and dances. Sometimes he sang with gospel quartets as he had as a boy. His only contact with the folks back in the Clarksdale area was by occasional mail. As fate would have it, he never saw any of them alive again.

Hooker's style is described as anywhere from undisciplined, simplistic and repetitive, to intuitive, heartfelt and primal. Hooker himself insisted that he could play "real perfect" if he had to—he just never felt that need. It simply wasn't him. Instead, he stayed true to his stepfather's code: "play from the heart and the soul." He may never have played a song the same way twice.

During the 1940's in Detroit, he worked as a janitor in the Rouge River steel works, playing guitar wherever he could, private parties as well as in bars. He found an audience in the many workers who had migrated north in search of work and longed to hear the music they grew up with. By the late 1940s, many small record labels were bringing various rhythm & blues artists to a wider audience, and soon Hooker was able to stop ushering and factory work and become a full-time musician.

A series of hits—*Boogie Chillen, Crawlin' King Snake, I'm In The Mood*—brought a growing popularity, and he recorded for a variety of labels down through the years, occasionally under aliases such as The Boogie Man. A long career brought Hooker fame, awards, tributes, and finally, in 1991, induction into the Rock and Roll Hall of Fame.

He has been called "the most African-sounding of all the major blues players of this century. . ." and reminds some of the traditional *griot* or African musical chronicler, who plays and sings the history of his tribe. Van Morrison called him "a shaman." B.B. King asserted that Hooker played the closest thing to "pure blues" he'd ever heard. Hooker says of himself, "My blues go so deep. . .teardrops run from my eyes." That surely echoes Will Moore's advice to play from the heart.

A song recorded in 1949, *Burnin' Hell,* shows the evolution in John Lee Hooker's own life metaphorically as it tells the tale of a man who, while asking for the prayers of the traditional church, still rejects their credo of heaven and hell. Similarly, he himself respected his preacher father, but knew he had to reject his father's narrower values in order to find the broader truth of his being.

That truth lay in music, and was nurtured by his stepfather, Will Moore. Hooker always believed in a Supreme Being, but one who would never send him to a fiery hell simply for expressing his musical soul. No, this God would doubtless say, as Hooker did in the lyrics of *Boogie Chillen,* "Let that boy boogie-woogie, Because it's in him And it got to come out." Which, all things considered, sounds a lot like Will Moore.

Gerald R. Ford, Sr. , stepfather of

GERALD R. FORD JR., President of the United
States, b. 1913

". . .whatever has been done by me in any way whatsoever. . .
is because of Jerry Ford, Senior, and Dorothy Ford."

Many people had no idea that the man who became
President Gerald Ford, Jr., was not by birth the son of Gerald
Ford, Sr. There were those who even commented on their
physical resemblance—big, outdoorsy types, who enjoyed
sports and hunting and weren't afraid of hard work. Besides,
what man would give his own name to a child he hadn't
biologically fathered?

The answer is: a man like Gerald Rudolph Ford, who valued
honesty, integrity, industry and compassion more than such
superficial considerations as who contributed the DNA. The
toddler whose mother he married was treated in all respects
like the three boys subsequently born to them, and was raised
with the same core values: work hard, tell the truth, and clean
your plate at suppertime.

Gerald Ford Jr.'s mother, Dorothy Gardner, met a wool
trader named Leslie King in 1912, and divorced him nearly as

quickly as she'd married him. Ford is a little vague as to what the problem was, probably because his mother preferred not to talk about it, but he alludes to quarrels and violence in the marriage. Although her life with Gerald Ford, Sr., was not always easy, it lasted over forty years through economic hardships, war, and all the lesser vicissitudes of life.

Gerald Sr. never finished high school but nevertheless did well for himself and his family. He started as a paint salesman, worked in the coal business with a nephew, and later owned his own firm, the Ford Paint and Varnish Company. Although they lost one house during the Great Depression, the family did comparatively well and was able to keep food on the table, retain domestic help (much cheaper back then), have a summer cottage, and keep company workers employed, albeit at a reduced income.

A scrupulously fair man, Ford paid himself what he paid his workmen, and somehow they all made it through the depressed years of the 1930's. If you gave him a good day's work, you were accorded the treatment of a member of his extended family. To Gerald Ford Sr., blood was not thicker than water. Fairness, decency and compassion trumped everything else, and his sons grew up believing the same.

It is not surprising that the Ford household produced two sons who spent at least some time in politics (brother Tom at the state level in Michigan). Politics and current events were frequent dinner table subjects, and both Mr. and Mrs. Ford were incredibly active in civic affairs, considering that they were concurrently running a business and raising a family. According to his son, Gerald Ford Sr. belonged to at least three fraternal organizations as well as being an ardent supporter of the Boy Scouts. He served as director of a project that provided recreation for disadvantaged youth. Not content to simply oversee at a distance, he saw to it that Ford Paint & Varnish contributed free supplies for the construction of a summer camp on the outskirts of Grand Rapids, and may even have wielded a paint brush.

Ford, Sr. also served as county GOP chairman, and he and Jerry were active in a progressive political organization called

Home Front, whose objective was to open up the political process and make it more honest and inclusive. Many members were young professional people. Some were even female, unusual for that time.

All the Ford boys had nothing but respect for Gerald Sr. and frequently consulted him on important matters. One such occasion involved a football game between Georgia Tech and the University of Michigan. The Georgia coach threatened to forfeit if Michigan's black pass receiver were allowed to play. Jerry, Jr., a key player on the team, felt this to be grossly unfair and wanted to sit out the game in protest, but first he called his father for corroboration of his feelings, or at least for some direction. On this occasion, the elder Ford simply counseled his son to do as his coaches wished. Ford reports that he felt "unsatisfied" with this, asked the black player himself what he would advise, and was told to go out and help the team, which wasn't having a very good year. Ford took his teammate's advice with a vengeance, sending one particularly racist Georgia player off the field on a stretcher.

As a recent college graduate, Jerry was offered a job as assistant football and boxing coach at Yale. His father disparaged it as a dead-end job, but Jerry saw it as a possible springboard to Yale Law School and accepted it. Although Jerry didn't always follow his father's advice, he frequently sought it, as he knew his father would give him an honest opinion based on what he thought was best for his son.

When he was about seventeen, Jerry was working as a cook in a local restaurant, one of the many part-time jobs he held at his parents' insistence. The Fords' financial situation fluctuated during the period between World Wars, but their wanting him to work probably had as much to do with character building as anything else, though Jerry was already a reasonably good student and a star athlete. He recalls happy times spent fishing or tossing a ball around with his dad, but both elder Fords crammed an enormous amount of activities into their lives and Jerry was evidently expected to do the same.

Jerry's only contact with his birth father occurred that year. Leslie King was doing well enough to drive up to the eatery in a brand new Lincoln, although the only child support payments Jerry's mother had ever seen came from the kindness of his paternal grandfather, and when he died, the checks stopped abruptly. King seemed interested in little beyond the fact that his son was a good athlete. When he left, he presented the boy with $25, as if that made everything even. That night, the tough football player cried himself to sleep. Naturally, he shared this distressing event with his parents.

Ford reports developing a general philosophy for dealing with people during this period of his adolescence and young adulthood. Its optimistic central tenet was that we all contain more good than bad elements, and life is far easier when you emphasize the good. Perhaps he was able to carry this over to his natural father, who never played any further role in his life.

A friend once gave Ford an anonymous poem about the definition of success. It cited such criteria as winning the respect of intelligent persons, earning the approval of honest critics, finding the best in others, giving of one's self, and leaving the world a bit better place for your passing through it. It reminded him, he said, of his parents. Although he had risen to the highest office in the land, perhaps the entire world, to him, the greatest success story ever was that of Gerald and Dorothy Ford.

Gerald R. Ford, Sr. died in 1962. Fourteen years later, Gerald Ford, President of the United States, was at the Kent County, Michigan, airport, attending the unveiling of a mural depicting different moments in his career. This is how he described it in his autobiography, *A Time To Heal.*

> "I guess the name will be the *Gerald R. Ford Mural,*" I said. "It means so much to me because of the first Gerald R. Ford and his wife, Dorothy, my mother and father. I owe everything to them and to the training, the love, the leadership" — the tears welled up in my eyes and I had to pause to brush them away—"and whatever has been done by me in any way whatsoever, it is because of Jerry Ford, Senior, and Dorothy Ford. And that is what that mural will always mean to me in the years ahead."

The Ford men were known as "strong, silent types" — sportsmen, leaders, and not easily given to tears. The two men able to evoke that response from Gerald Ford, Jr. was the man who served as a role model for how to live, and conversely, the one who showed him how not to.

Arthur Meigs Godwin, stepfather of

BETTY FORD, First Lady of the United States, 1918

*"I loved Arthur Godwin, and now I was so happy
he and my mother were going to be married that I asked
if I could call him Dad. He said he'd be delighted."*

Some people, by a quirk of fate, become forever entwined in public memory with events that no one would ever have foreseen when they were children. Jackie Kennedy, for instance, raised in wealth and security, is enshrined as the archetypal grieving widow. And who, hearing the phrase "Betty Ford Center," does not connect that in their minds with addiction and suffering? And yet, Betty Ford herself speaks frequently of her "sunny childhood" and "wonderful girlhood" in Grand Rapids, Michigan.

Raised in relative affluence, Betty remembers a life of country club toboggan parties, football games, and joyriding in convertibles with the top down. She was planning to be a career woman, and of course she'd marry someday, but right now the world was one big party and she meant to enjoy it. With one exception, the worst that happened was when a friend of hers sneaked a live duck into the showing of a horror movie and pitched it from the balcony into a woman's lap, nearly sending the woman into cardiac arrest.

But when Betty was sixteen, she experienced tragedy for the first time: the accidental death of her father, asphyxiated while working on a car with the motor running. By the time Betty arrived home, he'd been taken to the hospital and pronounced dead.

As an adult, Betty lived for a time in New York and studied with the dance maven Martha Graham. Her mother's life took a new direction, too—she fell in love with a neighbor and old friend of the family, Arthur Meigs Godwin. Betty had always referred to the Godwins as Uncle Art and Aunt Leona.

Art, a successful banker, had retired at forty-five and indulged in his hobbies of reading and traveling. But during an automobile trip through Mexico, he and his wife were in a serious collision, which Aunt Leona did not survive. Art barely lived through the crash. Passing farmers dragged him out of a ditch, took him home with them, and patched him up as best they could with whatever medical supplies they could find. After a long recuperation in Mexico, he returned to Grand Rapids. Betty's family had visited him regularly, and her father had driven him to the hospital for his weekly therapy. In a sense, Art Godwin was already a member of the family. It had remained for one further act of fate to pull him all the way in.

Betty was elated. Her mother seemed happy as a schoolgirl. Betty had always liked "Uncle Art;" now she could call him Dad. The Godwins had been childless and Art found this quite to his liking, too.

Betty's mother, Hortense, entered into this new phase of her life with a vengeance, asking Betty to sell their house and all its furnishings, and have it done by the time she and Art returned from their honeymoon. They were taking a year-long trip around the world, so there'd be plenty of time. Nothing was going to keep Art Godwin from enjoying travel, especially not when he had a new bride to see the world with him.

When the couple returned from their honeymoon, all three lived in the Godwin house on Fountain Street. Occasionally, this made for some friction in the usually amiable household. Betty's artistic side found an outlet in producing fashion shows for a local store and also in teaching dance, but Betty's attachment to her "talented and enthusiastic" students meant spending one night a week in a black neighborhood. The friction, Betty says, was because her stepfather, "a generous-natured man, was in this one area narrow-minded. Tuesday nights it was always very quiet at the dinner table…." But evidently there was not enough friction to end the dance classes nor to cause any irreparable problems between Betty and Art.

The situation with Betty's choice of boyfriends was a little edgier. One in particular, a fellow named Bill Warren, seemed to set them off to the point that Betty lied about the relationship in order to continue it. His parents thought of Betty as a good influence and gave their wholehearted approval. Betty's parents, realizing that she was of age and able to make her own decisions, simply gave in to the inevitable and offered their home as a setting for the wedding. They never made another unkind comment about Betty's choice of husband, and, in fact, they bankrolled the honeymoon.

This first marriage was not to last. Deferred from service in World War II because of diabetes, Bill went into the insurance business. The couple moved to different locations as Bill tried to get established. Betty worked in a department store and taught dance again. At one point, they lived in an area that had retained so much of its rural flavor that she was able to shoot a rabbit from out of a window and then serve it up for supper.

Three years later, she knew this was not the life for her and decided to ask Bill for a divorce. But as she was writing him a letter to tell him of her intentions, his boss telephoned to say that Bill, while on a business trip, had fallen into a diabetic coma. No one was sure he would live.

For the next two years, Betty's life alternated between working herself into a stupor to avoid dwelling on how her life was playing out, and spending occasional weekends with her parents at their cottage on Lake Michigan. Art and Hortense made no hindsight comments about Betty's judgment or the lack thereof, they simply welcomed her home for these brief visits.

Miraculously, the man who had been at death's door started to come back to life. When he was himself again, Betty asked for the divorce and got it. She accepted a settlement of $1.00 and was ready to start all over again.

Enter Jerry Ford, a young lawyer Betty had known casually during her marriage. He asked her out for coffee. In that place and time, people in the midst of a divorce did not go out on dates. Ford wouldn't go away, and Betty found herself giving in to his persistence. Although her parents were surprised to meet the two of them entering a movie theater that they were just leaving, they recovered from their initial shock and became as fond of Jerry as they'd been disapproving of Betty's first husband. Jerry seemed responsible and substantial, and they felt safe leaving her in his care. When they married, the invitations read, "Mr. And Mrs. Arthur Meigs Godwin request the honor of your presence at the marriage of their daughter."

Things happened quickly after that. Jerry was elected to Congress, the couple moved to Washington, and Betty's mother died of a cerebral hemorrhage. When Betty became pregnant with her first child, her doctors feared a miscarriage and advised her to move, at least temporarily, to a more congenial atmosphere than harried and overheated Washington D.C. Betty spent several months with her stepfather at the Lake Michigan cottage. Jerry came out for long weekends whenever he could. Betty kept hoping for a daughter, whom she planned to name Sally Meigs Ford, after a beloved childhood neighbor she called Aunt Sally, and Uncle Art. When three sons in a row arrived, she gave up and christened the third boy Steven Meigs.

When Art Meigs died, he left the Fords a small inheritance. They discussed the best way to spend their little windfall. Surely Dad meant for them to be practical and pay off the house. But on the other hand, Art Meigs had been a traveling man, and despite nearly losing his life on a motoring trip, he'd spent his second honeymoon on an around-the-world cruise. Art had married for a third time, and, although he is buried in Grand Rapids, had died in Cannes, France. And so, perhaps in his honor, they spent the money on a trip to Europe.

Walter Robinson, stepfather of

PEARL BAILEY, singer, actor, b. 1918

> ### Spots
>
> There's a spot of earth I call Mama,
> And another one called Papa,
> And spots called Mickey and Mr. Walter.
>   One day I planted flowers
>   In each spot.
> There is a star up there I call Mama,
> And one for Papa, and stars for
> Celia, and Don, and Mr. Walter,
> And. . .
> Do I still know each face?
>   There's a spot in my heart.
>   I wonder, sometimes,
>   Why it aches so.

"I put my hand on [his casket] and helped the men to push, I guess.
The reverend said…'That's love.'
[A]ll I could think was, 'You bet it is, sir, you bet it is.'"

Singer/actress Pearl Bailey nearly always referred to her stepfather, Walter Robinson, as "Mr. Walter," but the oddly formal-sounding form of address was really a term of endearment and respect for someone who played a role in her life for 40 years, until his death in 1970.

Pearl grew up in Washington, D.C. As a child, she witnessed the recurring arguments between her parents that occurred every Sunday, as regularly as clockwork, right after church. She never knew what they were about—only that her mother, Ella Mae, would pack her bags, and then have to unpack them when the heat of the moment had subsided. One Sunday the bags never got unpacked, and Ella Mae and the children moved several blocks away.

Papa, as she called her father, would come around and bring groceries, but his visits usually engendered yet another argument. Pearl was convinced that Papa wanted to reunite the family, but Ella Mae was adamant.

A few years into the separation, Ella Mae made the acquaintance of Walter Robinson, who was unfortunate enough to be visiting one Easter Sunday when Pearl's father chose to drop by the house. Despite the ensuing scene, Robinson refused to be chased off, and eventually became Pearl's stepfather.

Pearl and Mr. Walter developed a close relationship. She remembers him as being strict, but not as strict as Mama. On one occasion, when Ella Mae was out of town, Pearl managed to get away with enough slacking off at school to get suspended. Pearl was "his baby" and knew it, and probably took advantage of his fondness, which did not sit well with her mother upon her return.

By and large, Mr. Walter was an attentive father—Pearl recalls him teaching her how to drive well enough in three days to get her license—and a devoted husband to Ella Mae for forty years. They died within a year of each other, she in 1969, he in 1970. Pearl was told that during that year between, he sometimes sat outside their house, in tears, as though unable to go inside and not find her there.

At his funeral, Pearl stood looking at the casket, and seemed to see it as symbolic of her entire family. "For a moment," she says, "everyone was in it—Papa, Mama, Mr. Walter. . .I cried out. I could hear myself—that one tortured sound for them all."

Mr. Walter was as much part of her family as her blood relatives, perhaps more so, because in that instant he served as the unifying factor for them all. Pearl describes the following scene as Mr. Walter's casket was being rolled out of the church:

"I put my hand on it and helped the men to push, I guess. A nurse came near me. I didn't need help, so I moved her hand away. All I could do was keep walking with my hand on the box. The reverend said, somewhere behind me, 'That's love.' As I went down the aisle toward the front doors of the church, all I could think was, 'You bet it is, sir, you bet it is.'"

Shortly afterwards, Pearl wrote the touching memorial at the top of this chapter to Mr. Walter, and all her beloved departed relatives.

E.B. White, stepfather of

ROGER ANGELL, baseball writer, b. 1920

"If I was influenced by anyone, I guess it was by my stepfather,
\ E.B. White. . . He suffered writing but made it look easy.

Not everyone is lucky enough to turn a favorite hobby into a money-making venture, but Roger Angell's lifelong love of baseball, coupled with his skill as a writer, led to his being called by some "our laureate of the pastime." Joel Connaroe of *The New York Times Book Review* put it, "The next best thing to being at a baseball game is reading Roger Angell."

Most of his baseball essays appeared originally in *The New Yorker*, the magazine where he otherwise worked as a fiction editor, and struck most critics as being truly ground-breaking work, possessing what Steven P. Gietschier, in the *Dictionary of Literary Biography,* called "a grace and elegance previously unknown in sports journalism. . ." Angell's distinguishing traits were a great respect for the game and the players; a "sharp eye for a significant, generally unnoticed detail. . .;" the ability to ask just the right questions to elicit interesting and pertinent answers; detailed knowledge of the game; and a graceful, perhaps even poetic, style. Perhaps most importantly, as expressed by Wilfred Sheed, in the *New York Review of Books*: "Angell was born to write about baseball; it consumed him, as artists are consumed."

Roger Angell was born in New York City in 1920, the son of Katharine Sergeant Angell, an editor on the staff of *The New Yorker*, and Ernest Angell, a lawyer. By 1929 their troubled marriage ended and soon thereafter, Katharine married E.B. "Andy" White, who also wrote for *The New Yorker*.

Roger and his older sister Nancy spent weekdays with their father and weekends, holidays and summers with their mother. They attended the best schools (Harvard and Bryn Mawr respectively) before World War II turned their lives upside down, as it did the rest of the nation. Roger entered the Army Air Corps and became the editor of its magazine *Brief*. Nancy married a serviceman and presented the Whites with their first grandchild. In 1942, Roger embarked upon his first marriage, which provided two more granddaughters.

After the war, Roger worked as a contributor and editor for *Magazine X* and *Holiday* magazine. In 1956 he was recommended for *The New Yorker* by his stepfather, who assured management that he had "a rather sharp editorial talent. . ." even if his experience had not been very extensive.

In the best sense of the word, Angell grew up in the shadow of a remarkable writer, who was his introduction to the art of wordsmithing. Angell describes this in his foreword to the Fourth Edition of *The Elements of Style*:

> "The first writer I watched at work was my stepfather, E. B. White. Each Tuesday morning, he would close his study door and sit down to write the 'Notes and Comment" page for *The New Yorker*. The task was familiar to him. . .but the sounds of his typewriter from his room came in hesitant bursts, with long silences in between. Hours went by. Summoned at last for lunch, he was silent and preoccupied. . .he rarely seemed satisfied. . .Writing is hard, even for authors who do it all the time."

And yet the finished product rarely showed the blood, sweat, toil and tears that went into its genesis, any more than did Angell's critically acclaimed works on baseball.

Possibly best known for his popular and enduring children's books (*Stuart Little, Charlotte's Web, The Trumpet of the Swan*), White was born in Mt. Vernon, NY, in 1899, and attended Cornell University. After several years as a newspaper reporter, he was hired by *The New Yorker*, contributing editorial essays, verse and a variety of other work. Contemporaries and friends were such notables as Dorothy Parker, Robert Benchley, and James Thurber, with whom he collaborated on a satire entitled *Is Sex Necessary?* "No one can write a sentence like White," Thurber said of his co-author, known for his clean but elegant style.

In 1939 White moved to North Brooklin, Maine, and wrote a column for *Harper's* magazine called "One Man's Meat," which concentrated on his experiences in rural Maine. The essays were collected into a book and published in 1942; critics called this his best book yet. He did not return to New York City until World War II had begun. Although a profound nature lover, who called *Walden* his favorite book, White still felt an attachment to New York City, which he called "a riddle in steel and stone." In 1949 he penned these eerily prophetic words:

"A single flight of planes no bigger than a wedge of geese can quickly end this island fantasy, burn the towers, crumble the bridges, turn the underground passages into lethal chambers, cremate millions. . . Of all targets, New York has a certain clear priority. In the mind of whatever perverted dreamer might loose the lightning, New York must hold a steady, irresistible charm."

White also wrote passionately on the topics of segregation (against it) and internationalism (for it). He was somehow able to take the broad view on political matters while writing about them from an entirely personal point of view.

In 1959 White edited a style manual (*The Elements of Style*) based on privately published notes compiled by one of his professors, William Strunk Jr. It has since become a standard text used in high schools and colleges across the country, and sits next to the computers of today's writers (or should). The core principles stated in the book were: be clear, be concise, and be natural. The latter, however, does not mean that one never revises or edits. Natural is not synonymous with sloppy.

White offered this commentary on his own writing in a 1929 letter to his brother:

"I discovered a long time ago that writing of the small things of the day, the trivial matters of the heart, the inconsequential but near things of this living, was the only kind of creative work which I could accomplish with any sincerity or grace. As a reporter, I was a flop, because I always came back laden not with facts about the case, but with a mind full of the little difficulties and amusements I had encountered in my travels. Not till The New Yorker came along did I ever find any means of expressing those impertinences and irrelevancies. . .

". . .sometimes in writing of myself—which is the only subject anyone knows intimately—I have occasionally had the exquisite thrill of putting my finger on a little capsule of truth, and heard it give the faint squeak of mortality under my pressure. . .

. . ."To write a piece and sell it to a magazine is as near a simple life as shining up a pushcart full of apples and vending them to passersby. It has a pleasing directness not found in the world of commerce and business, where every motion is by this time so far removed from the cause and the return, as to be almost beyond recognition."

In later years, White kept up a lively correspondence with many people, including his stepson. His letters to Roger ran the gamut from writing, to his wife's (Angell's mother) failing health and activities, to his interaction with his dogs and the wildlife he encountered in the country.

White's comments on Angell's written work show him to be much as one of Angell's own protégé's, Garrison Keillor, describes his mentor: "terribly generous with his praise and apologetic for his criticism." In fact, there is almost nothing in the way of criticism. He is unfailingly appreciative of Angell's written work.

Tales of country life abound in the letters. One charmingly told tale begins with the phrase "I'm the father of two robins and this has kept me on the go lately." White then relates the story of how he discovered two orphaned birds and began feeding them, even inventing a baby formula for them consisting of, among other things, chopped worms and orange juice. His stories are a wonderful combination of realism and whimsy, precise description and comic exaggeration. For example, the discovery of baby praying mantises in his plant room:

> "about fifty baby mantises emerged, loaded for bear—loaded, really, for aphids and other tiny pests. . .A baby mantis is about three-quarters of an inch long and looks exactly like a common pin that has six legs and a pair of tiny hands clasped in prayer. The ferocity of them is awesome. I produced a tiny fly from the bell of a daffodil and presented it to the hungry hordes. One of them leapt on it like a tiger making the kill—never saw such a bloodthirsty infant."

In one touching passage, he writes to Angell of his mother's battle with age and ill health:

> "Both of us, of course, are suffering from the onset of professional inactivity, or inadequacy or both, and in her case it is greatly aggravated by her almost-lost dream of writing another garden piece or two, so as to put a book together. She came down here with a foot-locker loaded with catalogues and garden books, and she has hardly been able to touch it. She hasn't quite given up but her spirit is badly cracked, and it is the saddest thing I have ever had to live with, to see her this way, after having done so much for so

many, and now unable to do a small thing for herself. I sometimes think I would give everything I own for one garden piece, one book, and one restored lady."

Overall, the tone of the letters from stepfather to stepson is crisp, humorous, and totally loving in an unsentimental way.

On October 1, 1985, in North Brooklin, Maine, E.B. White died of Alzheimer's disease. During his lifetime he had been awarded the gold medal for essays and criticism of the National Institute of Arts and Letters, a Pulitzer Prize special citation in 1978, and honorary degrees from seven colleges and universities. One suspects, however, that he might consider the best tribute to be that written by Roger Angell in his foreword to the fourth edition of *Elements of Style,* published in 2000, in which he simply but eloquently states his recognition of, and admiration for, all writers who strive to produce "the clear and almost perfect thought."

Jack McEdward, stepfather of

BLAKE EDWARDS, director, writer, producer, 1922

Jack often used young Blake as an extra in his films;
grown Blake used Jack as a production manager
in his television series and films.

Writer-director Blake Edwards, who was honored for Lifetime Achievement at the 2004 Academy Awards, is a jack-of-all-trades director. He worked in a variety of media and movie genres, and went a long way toward revitalizing the art form known as "farce"—defined as "light comedy depending on situation rather than character." If not for Edwards, says *Current Biography,* "The sight gag, the pratfall, and other hallmarks of silent film comedy might have become a lost art."

William Blake Crump of Tulsa, Oklahoma, might never have achieved this: first he had to be transformed into Blake Edwards, scion of a show business family that reached back to the silent film era.

In 1926, little Blake Crump's mother married assistant director and production manager Jack McEdward and moved to California. Blake spent a lot of his childhood on film sets. His step-grandfather, J. Gordon Edwards, had started as a stage actor and directed his first movie for Fox Pictures in 1914. Thereafter, he directed all of the studio's major productions and worked frequently with superstar of the day, Theda Bara. He was promoted to production supervisor and worked until his death in 1925—just about the time step-grandson Blake arrived on the Hollywood scene.

Stepfather Jack McEdward cast Blake as an extra whenever he could. After graduation from Beverly Hills High School, Blake began playing bit parts for whatever studio was casting. After World War II and a stint in the Coast Guard, Blake was back in show business as both an actor and a screenwriter.

In 1949 he tried his hand at radio, creating the series *Richard Diamond, Private Detective,* and was soon writing other radio dramas and movie scripts ranging from fluffy musical comedies to the occasional more substantial drama.

It was ten years before he was directing movies that received real critical praise. 1958 and '59 saw the premieres of TV series *Peter Gunn* and *Mr. Lucky,* created by Edwards with suave heroes and jazzy musical scores which were subsequently much imitated but seldom equaled.

Edwards really came into his own in the '60s, with such critical, and popular, favorites as *Breakfast at Tiffany's, Days of Wine and Roses,* and the hilarious *Pink Panther* series, which established him as one of Hollywood's premier directors. At times, he was even able to handpick his own crews, and worked with both his stepfather and his uncle, Owen Crump.

The year 1965 marked the beginning of the first decline in Edwards' up-and-down career. By 1972, tired of studio meddling and loss of artistic control, he packed up and left for Europe with wife Julie Andrews, hoping to write something that would favorably display her talents. That ran into a brick wall of disapproving critics.

In 1974 he co-wrote, directed and produced *Return of the Pink Panther,* and suddenly his career was back on track. Critics' and audiences' positive response to Peter Sellers as the bumbling Inspector Clouseau gave rise to two sequels, each grossing more than the last.

Lured back to Hollywood by promises of total artistic control of his pictures, Edwards developed and directed three movies (*10*, *S.O.B.* and *Victor/Victoria*) which combined all of his stylistic trademarks: deft juxtaposition of intelligence and hilarity, drama and slapstick—and they all had meaty roles for Julie Andrews. As one reviewer said of *Victor/Victoria*, "the only depressing thing about it is the suspicion that Mr. Edwards is going to have a terrible time trying to top it." And he did. Later additions to the Pink Panther series never achieved the success of their predecessors and a 1995 Broadway revival of *Victor/Victoria* played to mixed reviews.

Edwards is described as a fan of jazz and mystery stories (which he was able to put to good use in his most successful TV series) and also as seeming younger than his years, which could be due to his practice of yoga and judo. Or perhaps it is simply due to an unflagging sense of humor and many happy years with "the beautiful English broad with the incredible soprano," as he said in his 2004 Academy Awards acceptance speech.

He was honored at the 1992 Cannes Film Festival, and in 1993 was given the Preston Sturges Award by the Writers Guild of America, West and Directors Guild of America. But the essence of Blake Edwards showed unmistakably at the 2004 Academy Awards, when he* flew across the stage in a runaway wheelchair, grabbed the statue, and then demolished a wall, in a brief but hilarious Dr. Strangelove Meets Inspector Clouseau kind of skit. It could almost have been written and directed by Blake Edwards.

* or a stunt double?!

Dr. Loyal Davis, stepfather of

NANCY REAGAN, First Lady of the United States, b. 1923

". . .my mother, Edith Luckett Davis. . .had a profound influence on the woman I turned out to be, as did her second husband, Dr. Loyal Davis, whom I have always considered my true father."

Gifted healer or arrogant and temperamental neurosurgeon? Political kingmaker or dedicated man of medicine? Aloof social lion or loving family man?

There is evidence that Dr. Loyal Davis of Chicago may have been a little bit of all of these things. But despite a long life filled with medical and scholastic achievements, he may be best known as the step/adoptive father of Nancy Davis Reagan, wife of the fortieth U. S. President.

When Nancy Robbins first met Loyal Davis, she had been living with her aunt and uncle in Bethesda, Maryland, while her mother, Edith, pursued a career in show business. This time was evidently happy enough, but young Nancy still longed to be with her mother.

Judging from her own later choice of career, one can only assume that she identified a great deal with her mother, and was quite happy when Mother announced to a pre-teen Nancy that she was getting married and Nancy would be coming to live with them. That is, if Nancy approved, they would marry. Because this would mean that they could all be together and be a real family, Nancy readily agreed.

That did not mean that she had no reservations about her new stepfather, and she admits to a period of mixed feelings while adjusting to the new arrangement. Dr. Davis, while being a decent enough parent, was at first just a means to an end, that being reunion with her mother.

The rather reserved and formal Davis found it within himself to be a loving parent. Shortly after Nancy's arrival in Chicago, his base of operations, he took her aside and offered to adopt her if she was agreeable. A man of principle, who adhered to a strict code of ethical conduct, he thought it would be inappropriate to do so as long as her biological father was alive, but nevertheless, he would if it was her wish.

At the time, it was not, but within a few years, she'd seen enough of "Dr. Loyal," as she called him, to pursue adoption on her own, with the help of a retired judge who lived in their apartment building. Illinois law permits a child over 14 to make an independent decision regarding adoption, so young Nancy set out for New York to obtain legal permission from her birth father, whom she refers to rather formally as "Kenneth Robbins." The terms "Dad" and "father" are invariably reserved for Dr. Davis.

Nancy's mother had kept in touch with her ex-husband throughout their separation, and Nancy paid him and his second wife intermittent visits, but for the most part, the Robbins side of the family was totally written off by Nancy. After an incident involving what she considered to be verbal abuse of her mother, and an ensuing argument that upset Robbins so badly that he locked Nancy in the bathroom, she threw her lot in completely with her mother and new father, even refusing to attend her paternal grandmother's funeral. She was a Davis now and determined to be *only* a Davis.

This man, who was to figure so prominently in the life of an American president, was born in Illinois, in 1896. Davis attended Knox College and later earned both an M.D. and Ph.D. at Northwestern University, where he later headed the Department of Surgery for thirty-one years. He also held important positions with the Chicago Surgical Society, American Surgical Association, American Board of Surgery and Neurosurgery, and the American College of Surgeons, and helped edit the ACS Journal for many years. He was a prolific writer of textbooks, novels, and scholarly articles as well as a bit of an inventor. This talent came to the forefront during World War II, when he developed a treatment for high altitude frostbite and a special protective helmet for air crews.

Loyal Davis has been described as brilliant, distant and emotionless except for noteworthy bursts of anger, strict, hard to work for, traditional to the point of being old-fashioned, and a bit obsessive, all of which was probably true, and to an extent these traits are acknowledged by his stepdaughter. But, to her, he was also "a man of great integrity," who was "gruff on the outside, but warm and tenderhearted underneath. . ."

After being allowed to actually watch him perform an operation, Nancy's pride knew no bounds. "Here was this wonderful, handsome, accomplished man—and he was my father!" she enthuses in her autobiography. At one point, as an adult, she even remarked to someone that she had "surgeon's hands" like her father—a logical impossibility, but indicative of the extent to which Nancy identified with this man, who embodied to her nearly all that was excellent and worthy of emulation. He may have made his subordinates cringe with his insistence on total silence in the operating room coupled with a tendency to throw things when someone irritated him, but his daughter remembers a man who wrote poetry for her and slipped it under her door, and sent her "silly limericks" when she was grown and away at school.

There seems to have been a whole side of Dr. Davis that was seen only by close friends and family. Just as his daughter, who had started her life traveling from theater to theater with her actress mother and took up acting as a profession, longed to be seen as the kind of "lady" her father would approve of, Loyal Davis had a lifelong urge to somehow be part of show business. His talents lay elsewhere, but many of his associates were connected to Hollywood, and he counted actor Walter Huston, called "Uncle Walter" by Nancy, as one of his closest friends.

Davis could never understand why actors commanded astronomical sums of money for simply reading words other people had written, whereas he, who actually saved lives, earned far less. One day he and Huston determined to make a recording of Othello for the amusement of their wives, with Nancy playing Desdemona, and even his adoring daughter had to admit that her father shouldn't give up medicine for acting.

Davis was not shy about using his Hollywood contacts to further his daughter's career whenever possible, starting with her screen test. Although he had been unable to cure Spencer Tracy's son of his deafness, Tracy was grateful enough for Davis' counsel in the matter to contact his friend Dore Schary, Vice President of Production, who saw to it that MGM's best technicians worked with Nancy on her test.

Davis seems to have made the same impression on Ronald Reagan that he did on Nancy, and eventually became a friend and supporter of Reagan's. Some claim to see the political ideas of Loyal Davis in Ronald Reagan, as though he had somehow "converted" Reagan from his staunch Democratic family background to Davis' own conservatism. Nancy is quite clear in her writings that no such thing happened. Dr. Davis insists that he did no more than offer opinions when asked. He may have had secret aspirations to show business, but he had none to politics, and hated the thought of his son-in-law entering this "sea of sharks." Still, he was supportive of Reagan once it became clear that this was to be his direction.

The future President's political opinions had drifted to the right long before he met Davis, but it is possible to document increasing references to the dangers of socialized medicine in Reagan's speeches. If the doctor was not the source of these sentiments, he certainly encouraged them.

Actress Lillian Gish reportedly told Edith Davis that her daughter would marry Ronald Reagan and it would undoubtedly be a happy and successful union because he and

68

Loyal Davis were so similar—they even looked alike. More importantly, both men had strikingly similar backgrounds, having come from small Midwestern towns and risen to positions of greater affluence than their parents. Both had been encouraged by dominant mothers to do better than their fathers, and had learned both to make money and to hold onto it, resenting any attempt by government to spread "their" wealth around.

Loyal Davis was hospitalized for the last time in 1982, at age eighty-six. Despite his written wishes, his daughter fought bitterly with the attending physician over his treatment. Davis wished to die at home. Nancy detested the thought of his dying at all and spent hours at her father's bedside begging him not to leave her. A lifelong agnostic, Davis called for a priest in his final moments, which might never have taken place had he not been urged repeatedly by his son-in-law to make his peace with God.

Some will always believe, as did the Davis' family physician, "….make no mistake about who converted Reagan." If so, Loyal Davis, in his own way, played a great role in the direction the United States would take in the latter half of the twentieth century. And the linchpin on which it all turned was the relationship between both men and Nancy Robbins Davis Reagan.

Albert "Tom" Harris, stepfather of

ERMA BOMBECK, humorous writer, b.1927

"My stepfather paid for all my needs and my whims, was there through all my growing up—and checked himself out of the VA hospital to give me away at my wedding."

Erma Bombeck knew she wanted to be a writer, no matter what anyone said, even her mother. Mom (also named Erma) thought it sounded boring, but Erma Jr. even loved the sound of words, and would often read aloud to herself for amusement after she got home from school. Mom wasn't around to hear— she was working in a General Motors plant, an extremely unusual state of affairs in Dayton, Ohio, in the 1930's. But the widowed Erma Fiste needed the money, and perhaps the space, as she had gone back home to live with her parents after the death of her first husband. The family home was inhabited by ten people across three generations, and money was always a concern.

Not long after taking the job with General Motors, Erma met and married Tom Harris, a co-worker, and they moved into their own home. This did not sit well with Erma Jr., who evidently felt displaced in her mother's affections and took it out on her new stepfather quite regularly. Their disagreements continued, with Erma Sr. often caught between the warring pair, until Erma Jr. found an outlet for her energies that diluted the hostility: writing for the Emerson Junior High newspaper, *The Owl*. Erma was a good student but not very socially oriented. Writing for *The Owl* became a major focus of her life and she soon developed an acerbic style that on occasion nearly got her expelled. But Erma was happier now that life held a goal: becoming a newspaper reporter.

That goal was not to be achieved overnight. Over her mother's objections, Erma's went away to the University of Ohio; Tom "lugged fifteen pieces of luggage" up to her third-floor dorm room. One professor was scathing about her writing. When she decided to leave school, her mother encouraged her to come back home, but the three were still not able to settle into a comfortable arrangement.

Erma soon enrolled in the University of Dayton, a Catholic institution, once again in pursuit of a writing career. She also simultaneously worked at a department store, an ad agency, and the YWCA. At least the department store offered her the opportunity to write—the company newsletter. This time, one of her professors recruited her to write for the University of Dayton's magazine, *The Exponent*, and encouraged her to pursue the career she wanted.

Upon graduation, Erma took a series of big steps: she became a Catholic, married Bill Bombeck, who was Catholic, and took a staff job with the *Dayton Herald-Journal*. The switch from Protestantism was with a few specific reservations. The job was not exactly to her taste either: writing obituaries did not come naturally to one with her natural sarcastic and comedic bent, but she was a journalist. In a later article, she gave kudos to Tom Harris for signing himself out of the Veterans Administration Hospital to give her away at her wedding.

College courses had provided some added insight in her earlier work, but fifteen years of marriage and motherhood provided Erma with a wealth of material for her first book, *At Wit's End*, which was published in 1967. It was not an immediate blockbuster, but remained in print, and providing royalties, for decades. Erma was on her way to the big time. She became the queen of what she called "utility room" humor, which dealt with the minutiae of reality: "screaming kids, unpaid bills, green leftovers, husbands behind newspapers, basketballs in the bathroom."

Erma seems to have conflicting memories of her birth father, perhaps because she was only nine when he died. She reports that as a child playing with dolls, she never knew what to do with the Daddy Doll, so she sent him off to work and played with the other dolls. In her piece, *Stepfather*, written in 1980, she writes in glowing terms of the people who find themselves in the middle of ongoing family situations and manage to keep life moving along in spite of resentment, recriminations and general awkwardness. There are frequent references to the discipline her stepfather saw the need for, but that young Erma found intolerable at the time. In retrospect, she insists that her birth father would never have provided that solid a foundation for her.

And yet, in her column, *Daddy Doll Under the Bed* (6/21/81), she tells of a man whose absences might have seemed mysterious to a small child, but who performed countless small thoughtful services for his family, took his daughter fishing, and even attended pretend tea parties. She admits that his passing left a deep hurt in nine-year-old Erma, one that went far past the fact that creditors immediately descended upon the family and carted off so many of their possessions that it was necessary to move in with Grandma.

Interestingly enough, Erma recalls her birth father teaching her to ride a bike. But by 1987, in *Family: The Ties That Bind. . .And Gag!*, she attributes this to her stepfather. Perhaps this is poetic license, perhaps unclear memories from fifty-plus years in the past—or perhaps a gradual acceptance of Tom Harris as her father so that many "daddy memories" blended together. By 1991, in *When You Look Like Your Passport Photo, It's Time to Go Home*, she's referring to Harris simply as "my father."

Harris was an undemonstrative man not much given to any overt displays of affection. Communication, to him, meant giving orders, issuing instructions, or setting boundaries for young Erma's behavior. If he asked questions, it was where she would be, who she'd be with and when she'd be home. At the time, she found this cold and intrusive. Later on, she decided that was merely his way of being a caring father, and learned to value this somewhat reserved man in a way she had been unable to do as a child.

The Harrises had always enjoyed travel, and Erma felt they should be able to take exotic vacations as long as they could walk onto an airplane, even if that meant the entire family would have to travel together. So that was what they did: the four of them experienced everything from bullfights in Spain to canoeing down the Amazon. Tom Harris kept up as well as he could, but frequently stayed behind while the rest of the quartet went on to whatever destination was the goal of the trip. Sometimes they left him on a park bench or in a village square, and learned upon their return that the world had come to him and provided as much adventure as they had encountered in their wanderings.

One afternoon he was "entertained by a snake charmer, treated to a political debate, and hit on by two hookers." She notes that he never snapped a picture to be enjoyed later—he was far too busy enjoying the present moment. Erma once wrote that she hoped she would be able to say, at the end of her life, that she'd left no dreams unfulfilled, no talents unused, and no love unspent—by inference, that she too had lived fully enough to have no time or need for snapshots.

Tom Harris died in 1990, a scant six years before his daughter Erma, but not before she had realized that her stepfather was one of her best friends. Tom had been too busy living his life to document it, so his daughter did it for him, most notably in the wonderful *Stepfather* piece reprinted in *Forever, Erma:* "My real father. . .," she wrote, "was there all the time, and I didn't know it."

* You must read at least that whole column for yourself. The information here came from several of her books. It was difficult to keep to the subject and not read more and more and more of her books.

Hugh D. Auchincloss, stepfather of

JACQUELINE KENNEDY ONASSIS,
First Lady of the United States, book editor, 1929

"[Y]et, to be fair. . .Hughdie was most generous to me; he gave me castles and toy soldiers. . .at Merrywood." Gore Vidal, stepson

If asked to succinctly describe the impression most Americans have of Jacqueline Bouvier Kennedy Onassis, two words might come to mind: glamorous and tragic. And yet this woman, who came to be the center of a family as close to royalty as America has ever had, might never have achieved that position without her stepfather, Hugh D. Auchincloss. Even those who knew him best and were inclined to speak most favorably of him described Hugh Auchincloss as generous, amiable, and dull. He and his stepdaughter were at opposite ends of the spectrum in many ways, and yet their association propelled her to the position that novelist Sarah Bradford characterizes as "America's queen."

The marriage of her mother, Janet Lee, to "Black Jack" Bouvier, to whom the newspapers referred as a "society broker," was probably doomed from the start. As early as their honeymoon, he was flirting publicly with other women and gambling himself broke. Jackie's recollection of the story is that her mother scraped together every penny she could find and won back all of his losses. Janet Lee Bouvier learned early on how to survive Black Jack's escapades, but never quite figured out how to deal with them emotionally.

She played the game as well as she could until Jackie was eleven years old. A sex scandal involving such a glamorous society couple was more than the newspapers could resist, and the resulting publicity around her parents' divorce made life very unpleasant for Jackie. Lacking today's blasé acceptance of such matters, her schoolmates tittered and whispered and no doubt laid the groundwork for what became Jackie's quiet and reserved public persona of later years. It was simply her way of coping.

Jackie and sister Lee spent about half their free time and six weeks in the summer with their father, who doted on the girls as the one bright spot in a life increasingly blighted by financial setbacks and personal losses, such as the death of his mother. He enjoyed taking the girls on such excursions as a visit to the stock exchange. A lifelong horseman, he loved watching Jackie taking prizes for horsemanship at local shows.

But everything changed in the summer of 1942 when Janet married Hugh Dudley Auchincloss. A lawyer and investment banker, "Hughdie," as he was known to familiars, was ten years older than his new wife and far wealthier than her former husband. Hughdie's grandfather had helped found Standard Oil and the Auchinclosses had all married well, with the result that the family eventually took up an impressive two full pages in New York's *Social Register.* Hughdie attended Yale and Columbia, worked for the Commerce and State Departments, and finally founded the Washington brokerage firm of Auchincloss, Parker and Redpath. The family owned two of the grandest estates on the East coast: Merrywood, a palatial home in McLean Virginia, and Hammersmith, a huge working farm with a twenty-eight room main house that resembled a hunting lodge with a spectacular view of Narragansett Bay.

Merrywood was home and the farm was the summer residence. Hammersmith was no gentleman's business write-off; it provided supplies to the American armed forces, so there was plenty of work to be done. The girls learned to cook and clean, tend the gardens, care for a variety of farm animals, and pick apples. Jackie loved both places but especially Merrywood for its pure rustic peacefulness, which she praised in many letters to her new stepbrother Yusha, Hughdie's eldest son, who became the older brother she had never had but always wanted.

Although her sister Lee referred to them as "my steps and halves," Jackie seemed to love having a crew of new relatives and her especially close friendship with Yusha that lasted for years. Even Hughdie's stepson, Gore Vidal, whose caustic wit spared no one, liked Jackie, speaking of her in glowing terms that many might find strange: "Jackie, whose boyish beauty and life-enhancing malice were a great joy to me. . .[was] a slyly humorous presence when she was in my life." Gore had been less accepting of Hughdie as a stepfather than Jackie. Neither could avoid comparing him to their natural fathers, both of whom were handsome, athletic, charismatic men.

Hughdie's best traits appear to have been that he was calm, respectable, amiable, and accepting—in short, an old-school gentleman. On the other hand, he was dull, unimaginative, stuffy, miserly, and tended to stammer when agitated. Perhaps to reduce the tension level, he sat quietly amidst the chaos when all the family was present, with his nose in a newspaper, while all the children (two with Janet Lee and three from previous marriages), and stepchildren (Gore Vidal and the Bouvier girls) and his wife conducted conversations, argued, or just generally lived their lives.

According to all his children, Hughdie tended to wilt in the face of Janet's temper, which often upset them, but if he never defended them, at least he never turned on them. For the most part, he seemed generally fond of his stepchildren, with the possible exception of Gore Vidal, whom he reportedly detested. Vidal, in turn, looked down upon Janet and at best found Hughdie to be a colossal bore. But it could not have been lost on Jackie that Hughdie's willingness to absorb and accept all the less than charming sides of her mother's character helped hold the family together.

At the same time, Jackie was trying to maintain some kind of relationship with her father, and found herself in the midst of yet another mixed family. Black Jack was conducting a rebound affair with a woman who had a young son, and they went on family outings to the beach, boating, or to watch Jackie compete in horse shows. Watching families come together, dissolve and re-form around her to such an extent taught Jackie that life was unpredictable and could be perceived either as an obstacle course or as an adventure. Jackie chose to see it as an adventure.

Even with all the activity in her new life. Jackie still found quiet time for reading, writing, drawing and simple contemplation. Hughdie's sister and brother-in-law were collectors of eighteenth century books and artwork and encouraged Jackie's interest in art and literature.

Jackie had always loved to write and contributed poems, articles and artwork to the school newsletter, which she helped edit one year. She wasn't entirely sure what she wanted to do with her life at this point, but she was sure what she did not want: to be a housewife. Ironically, her greatest fame was to come precisely from her association in the mind of the world as a helpmate to her first husband, John Kennedy.

In the private schools she attended, including Miss Porter's School in Connecticut, her talent as a clever mimic and language student became evident. She greatly enjoyed the drama club and wrote to Yusha that she would love to be an actress except that she had no desire to starve for the sake of art. The Jackie her contemporaries remember is not the gracious lady of televised White House tours but rather a witty, irreverent, even "raunchy" fellow student.

Contemporaries use words such as "different," "regal," "amazing," "standoffish," and "selective of her friends" to describe her. Jackie no doubt remembered her earlier school days when she became a laughingstock due to her parents' divorce scandal and so assumed something of an air of reserve to protect herself.

At age eighteen, Jackie endured the rite of passage of all well-brought-up girls of her social standing: the "coming out" ritual, in which wealthy debutantes were introduced to society via a series of balls and extravagant parties. Hughdie and Janet, with his money, spared no expense. Jackie was elegantly presented to society.

There were plenty of men around but no serious attachments. Jackie's love for her father, with whom she spent as much time as she could, was always tempered by a healthy awareness of his flaws. One former admirer said of her that ". . .she appreciated men but. . .liking them is another matter." By her own admission, she was interested in men with good minds and a strong character; yet she married a man who shared many of her father's shortcomings.

In 1948 a society columnist named her Debutante of the Year. She had absorbed so much of the Auchincloss society milieu that he was able to write of her: "Her background is strictly 'Old Guard.'" The real reason he chose her over possibly prettier candidates, was that "I felt something very special in her, an understated elegance. Although shy and extremely private, she stood out in a crowd. She had that certain something. I don't know precisely what word to use to describe this quality: beauty, charm, charisma, style, any or all of the above. Whatever it happened to be, she had it."

In the summer of 1948, Jackie took her first trip to Europe with the stepchildren of some of Hughdie's friends at the Treasury Department. She packed as much as she could into seven weeks of constant travel and sightseeing. The high point of the trip for this longtime history buff was meeting her hero, Winston Churchill, at a garden party, where she went through the reception line twice in order to see him and shake his hand an extra time. She thought this might be a once-in-a-lifetime opportunity.

Jackie had found Vassar College to be somewhat boring and persuaded Hughdie's brother-in-law to pull strings to get her into a group of Smith College students who were going to Paris to study at the Sorbonne. She lived with an aristocratic French family and learned to speak perfect French while she enjoyed the Parisian night life. She remained in close contact with her father by letter.

Jackie was determined not to return to Vassar. Her father pressed her to live with him in New York and work in his office, but Janet and Hughdie thought this a terrible idea. Janet felt it to be both a waste of her talent and too much time under her father's influence, and directed Jackie to George Washington University, which had a very reputable French department. Hughdie used his influence with acquaintances on the university's board and, despite a late application, Jackie was accepted.

Then another opportunity presented itself: *Vogue* magazine's annual Prix de Paris competition, with a prize of six months in the Paris office as a junior editor. Nostalgia for Paris surfaced, and Jackie prepared an outstanding submission, winning out over 1280 other applicants. Asked what notables she would meet if she could choose anyone, Jackie named Charles Baudelaire and Oscar Wilde, "...idealists who could paint their sinfulness with beauty and still believe in something higher." It was as though she were painting a picture of the man she would eventually link her life with forever—John Kennedy.

When Jackie left for Paris, she was accompanied by her sister Lee, whose trip was financed by Janet and "Unk," as the girls called Hughdie, as a graduation present. Thanks to Auchincloss connections all over Europe, the girls' tour of England, France, Spain and Italy was smooth and blissful, Jackie's stay at *Vogue* was anything but, and she left shortly after she arrived.

Eventually Jackie secured her place in history by marrying then-Senator Jack Kennedy in 1953. Conspicuously missing from all the festivities, from bachelor parties to the ceremony itself, was Black Jack Bouvier. First the Kennedys hosted a slam-bang party in Boston, followed by a more respectable, i.e. boring, Newport version hosted by Hugh Auchincloss at The Clambake Club, where Jackie had come out as a debutante.

Accounts vary as to the circumstances, but Black Jack Bouvier, who was slated to escort his daughter down the aisle, was too intoxicated to stand, let alone walk, so the honors were done by Hughdie. Some say that Black Jack, depressed over Janet's insistence that he not attend the prenuptial parties and dinners, simply drank himself into oblivion. Others say Janet had him forcibly detained in his hotel room to spare the family even the possibility of his showing up intoxicated. The newspapers were informed that he had fallen ill.

Jackie was devastated, but she held up well in public, later writing her father a note expressing her sympathy for how he had been treated. Her sister Lee, never on the friendliest of terms with their mother, called it "heartbreaking," and after the wedding, collected Black Jack and checked him into a hospital in New York.

The Auchinclosses remained close to Jackie and spent time with her during Jack's presidential campaign. They were sitting with her as the ballot returns came in. They even moved out of Hammersmith to another house on the grounds when the President and his entourage wanted to spend time there, and the farm turned into a huge family party. They were on hand for the important events, both sad and celebratory, in Jackie's life. After Jack's death, at Jackie's request, Janet and Hughdie slept in the President's bedroom the first night she spent in the White House as a widow. Years later, Hughdie escorted her down the aisle at her marriage to Ari Onassis, just as he had at her first wedding.

In 1975, Onassis died. Jackie had a residence in New York, near her children, and began work at Viking Press as a book editor. She worked there for years, resigned and began at Doubleday Publishing the following year. She worked as an associate editor, then full editor, then senior editor in 1982, working until shortly before her death from cancer in 1994. She is buried next to John F. Kennedy in Arlington National Cemetery.

In November of 1976, after years of ill health, Hugh Auchincloss died at the age of 79. Both Merrywood and Hammersmith had been sold to honor outstanding debts. By that time, Jackie was independently wealthy and able to provide for her mother, who had cared attentively for Hughdie in the years before his death and had also helped him pay off his firm's debts with money from her own inheritance.

Hugh Auchincloss stepped in at a difficult time in Jacqueline Bouvier's life and provided much-needed respectability and stability. Although he never achieved, or indeed sought, anything like Black Jack Bouvier's place in Jackie's heart, he certainly had his own place. It is somewhat ironic that having taken Black Jack's place in both of Jackie's wedding ceremonies, during the one grand and tragic ceremony in which Jackie Kennedy's face and demeanor were etched permanently into the American psyche—John Kennedy's funeral—the riderless horse representing the fallen hero was a beautiful, coal black steed named—what else?—Black Jack.

Ted Andrews, stepfather of

JULIE ANDREWS, singer, actor, author, 1935

"The next thing I knew, a personality as colorful and noisy
as show business itself—another Ted—came into my life.
He thundered across my childhood."

Julie Andrews—born Julia Elizabeth Wells just outside of
London, England—would eventually become familiar to most
of the English-speaking world as the face and voice of Mary
Poppins and *The Sound of Music's* Maria von Trapp. The dark
side of this instant and worldwide recognition was that she
became strongly identified in the mind of the viewing public as
the sweet, virginal, nun-become-mother-figure or the straight-
laced English nanny with a carefully tempered warmth. The
result was a career as full of mountains and valleys as the von
Trapp family's Austrian Alps.

Julie's father, Ted Wells, was a teacher of metalworking and
woodworking, and her mother, Barbara, gave piano lessons and
provided music for her sister's dance school. According to Julie,
her mother gave up a promising career as a concert pianist to
first help raise her younger sister Joan, and later to help Joan
conduct dance classes. In return, Joan gave Julie parts in school

productions and started exposing her to public performing at an early age.

In 1939 Barbara took a job as pianist at a seaside music hall, sharing the bill with a Canadian guitarist and singer named Ted Andrews. Simultaneously, Ted Wells went to work in a factory, where he met Winifred, an attractive young lathe operator. Before long, Ted and Barbara were divorced and starting new lives with new partners.

Julie and her brother were hardly affected, because their parents had a fairly amicable divorce and because they had been sent to the country for safety during World War II's intense bombing raids on London—that is, until it actually came time to go to live in the newly divided households. John lived with his father, but Ted Wells felt that Julie's obvious musical talent would be better nurtured in a more theatrical household, so she lived with her mother.

Julie took an instant dislike to Ted Andrews, but tolerated him because of her intense devotion to her mother. She relates that every time she visited her father, it was harder to go home. The Andrews family moved several times as their finances improved, but one thing all their wartime homes had in common was that there was always an air raid shelter nearby. Ted Andrews helped boost morale by leading community sing-alongs while the bombs fell. He began giving Julie singing lessons, partly to make friends with her, partly to go along with the ambitions her mother had for her.

By the time Julie was eight, her stepfather realized that she sang with unbelievable power for her age, and sent her to a throat specialist to be checked out. It was determined that this unusual child had a larynx as fully developed as that of an adult, as well as an incredible vocal range of four octaves.

Ted was elated and immediately sent her off to study with his own voice coach, Madame Lilian Stiles-Allen, with whom Julie developed a close and lasting relationship. "It's thanks to her that I didn't do more damage to my voice with all that singing when I was young…." Julie says. "I would take lessons twice a day. She had an enormous influence on me. She was my third mother." Her second mother, presumably, was her stepmother, Winifred Wells, with whom she developed an amicable relationship.

From Madame Stiles-Allen she learned to think of her voice as a gift to be carefully cultivated so it could be shared with others. From her stepfather she learned to work hard at a craft she was beginning to loathe. Although she resented Andrews for it at the time, in later years she was glad he had been such a disciplinarian, because it helped her develop an identity. "Without it I would have been ten times more mixed up than I was," she states. Because they both had such powerful voices, many who were not acquainted with her background assumed that Ted Andrews, whose name she now carried for ease of billing, was her biological father.

At the end of the war, Julie joined her parents' vaudeville act, which her mother admits was both for Julie's musical development and to bolster the act itself. Ted's show business connections paid off and Julie began working steadily on radio, television, and the stage.

Her salary went into a trust fund and Julie, who had no idea how much money she actually made, received an allowance of about a dollar a week. While the money came in handy, Ted also turned down performances he thought would be too taxing for Julie.

He began correcting what he considered to be her visual flaws: buck teeth and a lazy eye that tended to wander at unpredictable times. Julie was being prepared for stardom. By her own account, she had adopted her mother's and "Pop's" attitude toward show business and thought she "was the luckiest girl alive." At thirteen, Julie became the youngest person ever to give a royal command performance.

Julie, her mother, her stepfather and half-brother toured music halls all over the country, living in their own trailer to simplify the search for accommodations. Sometimes she performed with her parents, sometimes as a solo act. Her education was handled by a governess and a chaperone until she was fifteen, and her mother handled the press.

Tony Walton, a hometown boy, became a fan after seeing her in a stage production of *Humpty Dumpty*. She and Walton later married, though during this period, she had no time for anything but her career, which began to take off as her parents' were winding down.

Gradually, it became Julie who was largely supporting the family and putting her two half brothers through school. She took this responsibility quite seriously and the seeds were planted for becoming a lifelong workaholic.

Reports vary, but it seems certain that at least Ted Andrews, if not Barbara as well, was a serious alcoholic. Julie had difficulty acknowledging this. As a child, she filled diaries with fictionalized accounts of her idealized home life. Accounts of her personal life given in interviews throughout the years present a far rosier picture of life in the Andrews family than friends and acquaintances remember.

Decades after the fact, she sought psychiatric help to deal with her repressed feelings, but the only therapy available to her during the chaos was to spend as much time as possible with her father. Ted Wells led a far more relaxed and relaxing life than the Andrews, and Julie refers to the man she called Dad as "the wisest and dearest man I know."

Julie was introduced to an American audience in 1954 in a play called *The Boyfriend*, in which she'd starred in England. *My Fair Lady* followed in 1956. It fell to director Moss Hart to polish the diamond in the rough discovered by Ted Andrews until she could shine as brightly on stage as her seasoned co-stars. Julie remembers this as the "Days of Terror," but the extra coaching paid off. Audiences cheered and critics raved. In 1960, *Camelot* played to mixed reviews but Julie shone in the role of Guinevere, which she always claimed was one of her favorites.

Ironically, Warner Brothers' decision to cast Audrey Hepburn in the movie version of *My Fair Lady* left Julie free to take the role of Mary Poppins, which established her as a star of major proportions and garnered her an Oscar. (She even thanked Warner Brothers in her acceptance speech.) Then came *The Sound of Music*, which became the highest grossing film to date with the highest album sales. Critics were lukewarm about the film, but again loved Julie, who won another Academy Award nomination.

These were followed by a series of mediocre films but good personal reviews, which seemed to be a pattern in her career. In 1967 she was the country's #1 movie money-maker.

1968 proved to be a line of demarcation in Julie's career and personal life. Her first marriage dissolved, and in 1969 she married director Blake Edwards. Onscreen, nothing worked as intended and the same critics who had supported her earlier now deprecated her efforts to change her squeaky clean image by taking more earthy roles. One-woman shows in London and Las Vegas proved more successful. By 1979 more suitable, and better critically received, movie roles began coming her way, many directed by Blake Edwards (*10*, *S.O.B.*, *Victor/Victoria*). *Victor/Victoria* earned her yet another Academy Award nomination.

Julie's career extended well into the 1980's and 1990's and encompassed live performances, TV dramas, variety specials, and a short-lived TV sitcom. Her versatility, in fact, even extended to the writing of children's books. In 1995 she was nominated for a Tony for the Broadway revival of *Victor/Victoria*, but refused to accept it, as she considered that the remainder of the cast and crew had been wrongly and inexplicably overlooked. The talented little girl, who had passed from the hands of one kingmaker to another, was now confident enough to stand up and speak her mind to everyone in the industry. She was inducted into the Theater Hall of Fame in 1997.

The complete truth about Ted and Julie Andrews' complex relationship may never be known, but by the time Ted died of a stroke in 1966, he had laid the groundwork for his stepdaughter to launch one of the most successful acting and singing careers of the twentieth century.

Ramon Huidobro, stepfather of

ISABEL ALLENDE, author, 1942

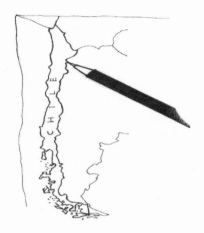

"I had never seen such an ugly man. . .he put up with all my contrariness without trying to buy my esteem or ceding an inch of his authority, until he won me over totally. He is the only father I have known, and now I think he is really handsome!"

Isabel Allende, born in Lima, Peru, was the daughter of a Chilean diplomat and niece of Chilean president Salvatore Allende, but in her own right, she became the first internationally recognized Latin American woman author. Although she spent time as a journalist, simple reporting was never her forte. Allende writes from the inside out: exterior events are never important in and of themselves, but rather for the effect they have on individuals for whom they are catalysts for personal growth. She might write with great authority of the Chilean coup d'etat of 1973, but to her, its true importance lay in the changed world-view of the young woman who came to realize that violence and uncertainty were everywhere.

Isabel's father had just abandoned his wife and three small children when Ramon Huidobro, another Chilean diplomat, literally walked onto the scene. Tio Ramon (Uncle Ramon) as the children called him, delivered the family back to the home of their maternal grandparents. Santiago, Chile was a colorful place during the life of Isabel's grandmother, a spiritualist who presided over "gatherings of intellectuals, Bohemians, and lunatics. . ." This ceased with her death, and the house became a far more cheerless place.

Isabel's mother did not lack for eligible men in her life, but kept up a correspondence with Tio Ramon, who was stationed in Bolivia. At last, fearing that one of Francisca's many suitors would transplant him in her affections, Ramon managed to return to Chile. His intense love for Francisca Allende led him to leave his own wife and children in order to care for her and her young family.

He confronted both her and her father. Neither man would budge, and so they reached a compromise: Ramon would move in with them so her father wouldn't have to worry about his daughter's whereabouts and safety, and in return he would have Ramon's marriage annulled. There was no divorce in solidly Catholic Chile, but people observed as many proprieties as they could. If he could not marry Francisca, at least he would not appear to be married to anyone else.

The children were immediately moved out of their mother's room to make room for Ramon. This marked the beginning of ten years of enmity between him and Isabel, who admits to a terrible jealousy she could not overcome. Looking back, she realized that, "He took charge of us children, just as he had promised that memorable day in Lima. He raised us with a firm hand and unfailing good humor; he set limits and sent clear messages, without sentimental demonstrations, and without compromise." He was to be the only real father Isabel would ever know.

Ramon had his own way of doing things and it differed greatly from Isabel's grandfather's way. Grandfather was rich, but he hoarded and skimped, whereas Ramon taught the children to enjoy what they had and find pleasure in unexpected places. Ramon bribed their way into the orchard of a nearby mental institution to pick apricots, surrounded by the patients, who terrified Isabel at first, but then just became part of the experience.

When neighbors verbally abused the children because of their mother's illicit relationship, Ramon tried to teach them not to care.

When Isabel was eleven, Tio Ramon was reassigned to Bolivia. The entire family of five left for LaPaz. The government would only pay to transport a legal family; Ramon paid for most of their expenses himself. Although Isabel loved much of her life in Bolivia, politically she began to see things through new eyes as she absorbed how others viewed Chileans, especially their armed forces. Not yet having experienced the brutality of revolution firsthand, she made herself unpopular by defending her countrymen.

In 1954 they were posted to Lebanon, where they spent three years in familial warfare. To say the consulate was small would be an understatement—it consisted of one room in the family's apartment in Beirut—and funds were always scarce.

As always, Tio Ramon managed. Francisca disliked the culture and the climate, but Ramon evidently adapted better than she. The pressures from without and within took their toll, and Isabel relates that they would argue "to the point of exhaustion."

Isabel, meanwhile, was in the full throes of her jealous hatred for her stepfather and tried her best to make life miserable for him, even plotting in her child's imagination to kill him in a variety of horrible ways.

Isabel attended a religious school whose best feature, in her mind, was that it kept her away from home. Being at home meant dealing with Tio Ramon, who "taught me by example and a methodology that modern psychology would consider brutal." He had been trained by Jesuits to be "intimidatingly emphatic and implacably logical. . ." and so became a formidable opponent in arguments with her mother as well as a stern teacher for Isabel.

Ramon decided Isabel needed to learn to think for herself and to never waver in her conviction, so he made her compose written defenses for both sides of so many arguments that she was later able to represent her school on the debating team. He also instructed her in arts thought more suitable to young girls in that culture. Isabel would have preferred to stay home, but Ramon encouraged her to attend diplomatic parties and overcome her fears of being a wallflower, even if it meant closing the consulate for an entire afternoon just to teach her how to dance. As he left her at her first party, he gave her a piece of advice she would never forget: "Remember that all the others are more afraid than you."

On one occasion, however, no one could have convinced Isabel that anyone, except her two brothers, was more afraid than she was. The three Allende children had learned how to raid Tio Ramon's locked wardrobe in order to pilfer such treasures as chocolates and cigarettes. Eventually they were discovered, and, with the help of one of his employees who posed as a policeman, Ramon played out a terrifying charade that convinced the children that they were all going to jail.

Also hidden in the mysterious wardrobe were four bound volumes of *A Thousand and One Nights*, which Isabel found to be fascinating reading, and which added to the love of storytelling she had already inherited from her mother and grandmother. "On those pages," she said, "love, life and death seemed like a gambol; the descriptions of food, landscapes, palaces, markets, smells, tastes and textures were so rich that after them the world has never been the same to me." Tio Ramon was unwittingly helping to set his stepdaughter onto the path she followed to international fame as a chronicler of Latin American lives and events.

As the political situation worsened in Lebanon, Tio Ramon became increasingly concerned for the children's safety, and sent them back to Chile. Ramon, with Francisca, was then posted to Turkey. Isabel finished school; worked as a secretary for the United Nations; took a job as a reporter, editor and columnist for a radical feminist magazine called *Paula;* worked part-time for a children's magazine; and took up television journalism.

Isabel had married at nineteen, finding that preferable to going to Switzerland with her parents when Ramon was named Chile's representative to the United Nations. Ramon suggested inviting Isabel's birth father to the wedding, but she refused, so President Salvatore Allende represented her father's family and Tio Ramon escorted her down the aisle. When Ramon and Francisca left for Switzerland, they had paid the first six months' rent on Isabel's new house and stocked the pantry with food to get the newlyweds off to a good start.

Motherhood did not come naturally to Isabel, who preferred working and leaving her daughter Paula in the care of her grandmothers. When she and her husband went to Europe, Tio Ramon stepped into the role of surrogate grandparent. Isabel describes his first meeting with his grandchild:

> "Tio Ramon has not been the inspiration for any of the characters in my books; he is too decent and has too much common sense. Novels are made of the demented and the villainous, of people tortured by obsessions, of victims of the implacable mills of destiny. From the narrative point of view, an intelligent, good man like Tio Ramon is useless; on the other hand, as a grandfather he's perfect. I knew that the instant I handed him his first grandchild in the Geneva airport and watched tenderness surface from a secret wellspring hidden until then."

Isabel and her husband slowly grew apart, but Tio Ramon remained a constant in her life and that of her children, whom he would dazzle with an endless series of imaginative pranks and games, such as pretending to call the President of the Republic of Switzerland and ask that the fountain outside their window be turned on especially for his granddaughter. Due to fabled Swiss punctuality, the fountain would spray exactly when it was set to, but the child was convinced that Grandpa was either a very, very important person or a magician.

In a school essay, Paula wrote that her "only interesting relative was Tio Ramon, prince and direct descendant of Jesus Christ, owner of a palace with uniformed servants and armed guards." Her teachers thought the child was unbalanced, until Tio Ramon drove up in a limousine with a motorcycle escort to pick her up for a dental appointment.

The fortunes of Isabel's birth father had diminished as Tio Ramon's had risen. When Señor Allende had a heart attack, his body was taken to the morgue by Public Assistance. Isabel's name was found among his papers, and she was called to identify the body. Thinking it was her missing brother Pancho, she called Tio Ramon for moral support, and they claimed the body together, at which time he informed her that the corpse was actually her father. Isabel felt more curiosity than grief and pursued the matter no further, despite soon discovering the existence of half siblings who, oddly enough, had been given the same names as Isabel and her brothers.

Tio Ramon's next diplomatic post was Argentina, considered Chile's most important after the United States. The world was examining Salvatore Allende's socialist experiment in Chile carefully, and in Argentina it was represented by Tio Ramon, who took his position very seriously. Relations between the two countries had been strained for years, so Ramon tried to be as open as possible to people from all strata of Argentinean society, to manage the budget with great care, and most importantly, to deconstruct the private security force which had become synonymous with hired killers, and in fact numbered an incredible 30,000 strong. Needless to say, this private army of virtual terrorists did not wish to be put out of existence, and during the next four years, Ramon and Francisca endured several bombings and other attempts on their lives. Despite this, Isabel's children, Paula and Nicolás, frequently visited their grandfather in Buenos Aires, and were given small jobs to do in Tio Ramon's office.

On September 11, 1973, a military junta overthrew the socialist government of Chile, assassinating President Allende. Isabel heard her uncle's last words on a radio broadcast. In Buenos Aires, Ramon settled affairs at the embassy, resigned rather than collaborate with the military junta, and began moving out. For all intents and purposes, his diplomatic career was over.

The political situation in South America, and especially in Chile, had become truly precarious for anyone associated in any way with the Allende government. With Allende's demise, terrorists were able to harass with impunity, and even murder, Chilean exiles who had been allied with the former government. Among their number was a good friend of Ramon's who was killed by a bomb placed in his automobile. Isabel did what she could to help victims of the junta survive, or escape, at times taking what she called "absurd risks" to do so. After receiving death threats, Isabel and her family reluctantly decided to leave Chile—if they could find a refuge. Many South American republics were closing their doors to Chileans because so many had already emigrated shortly after the fall of Allende. Through one of the contacts Ramon and Francisca had made in their endless travels, arrangements were finally made for both families—Francisca's and Isabel's—to move to Venezuela.

It was not a smooth transition for anyone. Isabel threw herself into countless love affairs and the children acted out their confusion with everything from tantrums to fighting and acts of vandalism. Tio Ramon intervened diplomatically when Nicolás assaulted a Venezuelan Senator with a raw egg, and provided whatever advice and comfort he could to Isabel. Despite his own family situation, he counseled her to try to hold her marriage together, but this was not to be. Her husband's work constantly took him away to remote job sites, and Isabel, bored and unfulfilled, could sometimes not resist the urge to flee with the lover of the moment, leaving her children to be cared for by their grandparents, or to raise themselves. Isabel's career in journalism came to an abrupt halt, as she was unable to find work in her field in Venezuela—she was, after all, an illegal political refugee without proper papers. After a time she was able to become a teacher. Earlier thoughts of writing were put aside and her life drifted.

In 1981 she began writing what she told herself was a long letter to her grandfather. It turned into her first novel, *The House of the Spirits.* A multi-generational story of a South American family told through a character based upon her grandmother, the book was a great success and typified the Allende style: a colorful story set in South America, revolving around the lives of one or more strong women characters, and while depicting real events in a realistic way, still recognizing the influence of the unseen world of passions, dreams and myths. "We know that there is a dimension in which we move constantly, and that is what in literature has been translated as magic realism," she explains.

Tio Ramon surprised her by obtaining a pre-publication edition of the book and presenting it to her before she left for Spain for the official publication. It had required twisting the arms or greasing the palms of editors, diplomats and ambassadors, but he accomplished this feat with the same seeming ease with which he had earlier transformed an embassy chauffeur into a policeman to threaten three thieving children. Tio Ramon simply knew how to get things done, and with flair.

At age 70, Tio Ramon decided he wanted to die in his native land, so he and Francisca returned to Chile. Isabel stayed in Venezuela, but her life was taking a new direction: she finally faced the fact that she wanted her freedom from her husband of 25 years. There were no recriminations. The children helped their father relocate and Isabel, finally free of her past, "began to dance and whirl like a maddened dervish." Tio Ramon arranged the usual conglomeration of lies and legalities known as an annulment in Chile.

The following years were a time of freedom spent in writing, teaching writing, and traveling. This freedom extended to her love life, of which she writes ". . .if a woman is available, there is no shortage of men." At first content to simply enjoy and observe people, considering everyone possible grist for the mill of her writing, she swung at last into the orbit of California lawyer William Gordon, whom she found fascinating enough to marry. He, like Tio Ramon, was not to be a model for a character in a novel. He was to be an anchor in her free-wheeling life.

Isabel no doubt recognized herself in one of her new stepsons, whose first statement to her was "I don't have to love you." Her reply: "Neither do I. We can make an effort and try to love each other, or just treat each other with good manners. Which do you prefer?" The boy decided they might try to love each other. "Good," she said, "and if that doesn't work, we can always fall back on respect."

Allende describes her life's journey as looking like "a plateful of noodles. . ." but noodles are slippery and bland. They may require a fork to impale them, or spices to enliven them. Life tends to provide this, but if it does not, one should see that it does.

"I've tried to make my grandchildren's lives as difficult as possible," she says, "so they will grow up to be creative adults." In other words, face your fears, stand up for yourself, and when you have the choice to sit it out or dance—dance. Had he been a writer, Ramon Huidobro might have expressed the same sentiments.

Miroslav "Mirek" Navratil, stepfather of

MARTINA NAVRATILOVA,* tennis player, 1956

"I'm proud that Mirek Navratil's family name is embossed on the trophies from Wimbledon and the other tournaments I have won. He was a father to me in every sense of the word, and it was his energy, his enthusiasm, that gave me my chance in tennis."

It is hard to write about Martina Navratilova without using superlatives. She has been described by tennis commentator Bud Collins as "arguably the greatest [tennis] player of all time" and by *Newsweek's* Curry Kilpatrick as "the best female athlete of all time, arguably." At the very least, others call her the best paid and most famous female athlete in the world. The *National Sports Review*, United Press and Associated Press named her Female Athlete of the Decade for the 1980's. The adverb "arguably" occurs frequently because it is undeniably difficult to assess such intangibles as relative fame: how would one realistically compare athletes competing in different fields?

Nevertheless, it is hard to dispute the numbers. When inducted into the International Tennis Hall of Fame in 2000, no one had ever compiled such impressive statistics: most singles tournaments, most titles, most matches, and nearly the most money won. The mildest praise bestowed on her defines her as, "For twenty years. . .a fearsome presence on the tennis court. . .by virtue of her powerful athleticism and brilliant tactics."

Martina Navratilova did not simply appear out of nowhere on the international tennis scene. She was the product of a family, indeed a nation, of tennis players. Her grandmother, Agnes Semanska, was a nationally known contender and her mother was also a lifelong sportswoman, although never exhibiting the talent of either her own mother or her daughter. Perhaps Jana Subertova simply didn't want it badly enough. Her daughter Martina did, discovering at an early age that tennis was what she enjoyed more than anything.

Martina's mother gravitated more toward skiing, perhaps because of the freedom it gave her from her father, who was evidently a physically abusive tyrant bent upon making a tennis great of his daughter, who, after a time, simply refused to pick up a racquet. Instead she became adept enough to become a ski instructor, where she met and married Miroslav Subert, head of the local ski patrol. In 1956, their daughter Martina was born, and by the age of two, the child was taking skiing lessons. Soon, Jana and Miroslav separated and she moved back to her home town of Revnice. Miroslav wasn't an entirely neglectful father, maintaining at least periodic contact with Martina until Jana remarried. Most of Martina's early childhood memories of him were pleasant enough, but the man who had the most lasting influence on her life was her stepfather, Mirek Navratil.

Tennis is to Czechoslovakia as baseball and basketball are to America—something of a national pastime. As soon as Jana Subertova moved back home, she joined the local tennis club. Czechoslovakia was not a rich country and many people earned their privileges by donating time and effort rather than paying money. This was the case at the tennis club, where members regularly performed all sorts of grounds maintenance. Little Martina, who characterizes herself as a "court rat," befriended a man who seemed to be working very hard to repair the clay court. He gave her wheelbarrow rides and brought chocolate for her every time he was at the club. Although she didn't know it at the time, he was to become her future stepfather. That was fine with Martina: by that time, they were already friends. She started calling him "Tato," the Czech term for Daddy, as soon as he and her mother returned from their honeymoon.

Martina and her family spent several years crammed into rather crowded living quarters (three to a room until the arrival of her baby sister made it four), but except for her unpleasant grandfather, everyone managed to get along. Mirek Navratil seemed to enjoy having a daughter old enough to be a companion to him, and the family turned into a cohesive unit that enjoyed all kinds of sports, berry picking, mushroom hunting and, in Martina's case, being pulled on skis behind Tato's motorcycle. Due to their refusal to join the Communist Party, neither Jana nor Mirek, both of whom worked, were able to enjoy the kind of lucrative careers they otherwise could have, but the family was comparatively prosperous. Still, the only real arguments Martina remembers concerned money.

Martina remembers her mother as a well-rounded person who was both an active sportswoman, a working woman, and a loving and nurturing mother. Dad was the disciplinarian, but hardly the bully her grandfather had been to her mother. For the most part, Mirek and Martina operated pretty much on the same wavelength, and he was her mentor and teacher in ways ranging from being her first tennis coach to explaining the "facts of life." When she was ten, she took the name that would become a legend in the world of tennis and officially became, not Martina Subertova, but Martina Navratilova.

At the age of four-and-a-half, she was slamming tennis balls against a brick wall with an ancient racquet inherited from her grandmother. Within a few years, Mirek was showing her how to play on a real court. Perhaps he sensed that this skinny but energetic child held a determination and innate talent that would extend far past her age and size; perhaps he was just sharing something he enjoyed with a child he loved. From the beginning, Martina knew that tennis was her game and soon fellow left-hander Rod Laver became her idol. Her mother played against Martina until Martina became skilled enough to beat her. Because of her own tyrannical father, Jana Navratilova was reluctant to push Martina. Mirek, however, was an unceasing source of encouragement, and would tell her to envision herself on the court at Wimbledon receiving the trophy. This may have been only a training device at the time, but it was a prophetic one.

When Martina was only nine, Mirek arranged for her to study with the best tennis coach in the country, George Parma, who at first glance thought Martina was a boy. It didn't take long for Parma to realize two things: Martina was a girl, and *she* was one of the best young players he had ever encountered. Martina developed a massive crush on her teacher and that, coupled with her innate passion for tennis, ensured that she would make the most of her time studying with Parma. Interestingly, Parma never took any money for the lessons. Perhaps he, too, realized that although he was famous at the time in Czechoslovakia, his eventual worldwide fame would stem in part from having coached this unusually talented child.

Between the two coaches, Martina's polished skill shone. She and her father attended countless tournaments, riding on his motorcycle because the family couldn't afford a car. At her first one, Mirek supposed she would merely be gaining experience, so they didn't pack enough food for a second day at the tournament. To his surprise, Martina won a match against a bigger, older opponent, so he had to motor all the way home for more supplies. After George Parma defected to the West, her father became her number one coach again, although Parma sent outlines and advice for her training.

Martina began to compete in Europe, and then all over the world. This was allowed because only her father accompanied her, the rest of the family had to stay home as unofficial hostages held against Martina's return. Always something of a free spirit, Martina became more and more enamored of the American lifestyle, and thus increasingly suspicious to the Communist officials who monitored and regulated the lives and careers of all Czech athletes.

When Martina was old enough to travel unsupervised, she stayed in contact with her family at least by telephone. She even acquired that most American of accoutrements, a business manager, who won her the right to keep even more of her ever-increasing winnings. One of the first things she did was to buy her parents a new car. Eventually, she bought them a house.

Increasing scrutiny by, and pressure from, the Czech tennis foundation eventually forced Martina's hand, and in 1975 she defected to the United States. According to the Czech government, her family was horrified. Martina's version was that her father had told her long before to do what she felt she must and to not pay attention to any resultant propaganda. He asked only that she be absolutely certain of her decision before she did anything. She never discussed this with her mother, whom she says asked her not to tell her if she intended to leave forever—Jana simply felt she hadn't the strength to deal with such an emotionally wrenching situation. So, without being able to say goodbye to anyone, at age eighteen, Martina simply packed her bags and left for the U. S. Open. For years, her main means of contact with her family would be by telephone.

By 1979, the Czech government relented and allowed the Navratil family to emigrate to America. Martina, then financially flush, bought them a new house down the street from her own. To her dismay, they announced that they wanted to live with her. There were two major problems with this: her family was unable to come to grips with the fact that their daughter was now an adult and not required to follow their directives about how to live her life, and they were totally unable to deal with her uncloseted homosexuality.

Only then, years after the fact, that they revealed to Martina that her birth father had not just died, he had committed suicide, and they feared for her mental stability as well. At this point, Martina was involved with well-known author Rita Mae Brown, whose candor about her own sexual orientation occasionally caused its problems for Martina. While the Women's Tennis Association was becoming increasingly homophobic and fearful for its players' reputations, Brown was pushing Martina to demand respect for her individuality, which also caused her to bear the brunt of the Navratil family's displeasure.

Martina and Mirek were having other problems as well: she realized that she had far outgrown his ability to coach her as a tennis player, and he was generally having trouble adjusting to life in the wide open Western culture of the United States. The friction increased until the Navratil family finally decided to return to Czechoslovakia.

Even so, Martina never doubted her family's deep underlying love for her, no matter how much they fought. Somewhere along the way, Mirek must have softened his stance on Martina's sexual orientation, because Martina reports that by 1984, her father so liked her current partner that he invited her to visit the family in Czechoslovakia.

Eventually Martina became a U.S. citizen and was allowed to return to her homeland for visits and to play in tournaments, where she was cheered wildly and besieged for autographs, having become something of a national hero. Although hoping to extend her career until age forty, Martina reluctantly retired in 1994 after the ascension of Steffi Graf, Monica Seles, and a new generation of tennis superstars. She lives in Aspen, Colorado, and spends a great deal of time working for non-profit groups such as The Sierra Club and The Women's Sports Foundation.

Her spectacular rise to fame might never have come about had it not been for Mirek Navratil. As Martina says, "My second father—I never called him my stepfather—always reassured me that my time was coming. . ." When it did, the wiry little kid who used to beat older and stronger opponents burst onto the international scene like a Czechoslovakian comet and went on to become "one of the world's most successful, colorful, and controversial athletes. . ." of all times.

Unarguably.

* -ova is the suffix that shows the last name is a woman's.

Bob Brandt, stepfather of

JAMIE LEE CURTIS, actor, author, 1958

"My stepfather, who raised me since I was a little girl, is Daddy, the one I go to with dad problems. He has always been around and supportive — a complete papa."

Jamie Lee Curtis, the daughter of one of Hollywood's elite show business couples, says she had the longest middle name of anyone she knew: Jamie Janet-Leigh-and-Tony-Curtis'-Daughter Curtis.

Sometimes called "the Tom Cruise of his generation," Tony Curtis' film career included roles ranging from a cross-dressing musician (*Some Like It Hot*), to the lead in *The Boston Strangler*. Janet Leigh was immortalized in the mind of the public as *Psycho's* shower victim. Their seemingly stable marriage collapsed after 10 years and two children. Before long, both had remarried, Leigh to a handsome stockbroker/occasional movie director named Bob Brandt.

Of her relationship with Tony Curtis, Jamie says, 'My father was sort of a stranger, then a real stranger, then an enemy. Now he's a friend." In the meanwhile, Brandt was playing the role of live-in daddy, and he evidently did it well. The family lived as unostentatiously as possible in Benedict Canyon in an effort to give the girls (Jamie Lee and Kelly) as normal a childhood as they could.

Bob accompanied the children on outings to Disneyland, took the family white water rafting and water skiing, and drove the girls around to visit friends on a motorcycle with a sidecar. Janet Leigh was careful not to make the girls feel that their father was being supplanted, but rather that the family was being added to. As youngsters, they would tell friends they had two daddies, one of whom was "Daddy Bob."

Jamie was miserable as a teenager. No matter how she and her parents tried, she always felt she stood out from everyone else, and her dearest wish was just to blend in. She describes those years as "a killer," a time when she would fish in the lost and found box at school for old clothes, which she would substitute for the expensive wardrobe she had worn to school. When Janet Leigh moved to New York City to do a role on Broadway, Jamie attended Choate, an exclusive prep school in Connecticut, where she found it harder than ever to disguise her Hollywood style. "It was a nightmare," she said. "I've never been so depressed."

After an abortive attempt at college, Jamie auditioned for a part in an upcoming TV series based on the Nancy Drew books. She didn't get a part, but she had been noticed. Television roles started flowing in regularly. Desperate to establish her own identity and worth, Jamie accepted the lead role in a relatively low budget horror movie that was to change her life.

The movie was *Halloween*, which reached the status of cult favorite or classic, depending upon how you feel about the film. It is indisputable that *Halloween* has been imitated more than most, spawned several sequels, and grossed over $100 million (of which Jamie was paid $8,000). Part of Jamie was so lacking in self esteem and sense of identity that she became, in her own words, "a chameleon" who resembled what- and whoever was around her.

But something in her still yearned for its own identity, and when *Halloween* was released, she insisted on the billing,

"Introducing Jamie Lee Curtis," which she thought sounded more individual than "starring."

Halloween was my deb party," she says, and it did introduce her to the world. In the next two years, she appeared in four more horror films, one after the other, including *Halloween II*, and quickly became known as "The Queen of Screams." Ironically, she claims to hate the genre and says she neither watches such movies nor understands those who do.

To escape the image, she held out for different types of roles, and found them, including a smallish supporting role as a hooker in *Trading Places* (1983), which won her the British equivalent of an Oscar. The Scream Queen was now a bona fide actress, or so she thought, but her next series of films all seemed to feature so much nudity that she acquired a new nickname: "The Body."

She was drawn to drugs, and admits to becoming a user, although she refuses to call herself an addict. Drug use became a common ground for Jamie and her estranged father, who was addicted. When she decided to break her habit and he could not stop, they parted company for the second time in their lives. In 1984, she married comedian Christopher Guest, and seemed poised for stardom.

After a 1984 flop (*Perfect* co-starring John Travolta), the roles she wanted eluded her until a successful 1988 comedy, *A Fish Called Wanda*, where she played a role written especially for her. In 1990 came TV series *Anything But Love*, for which she won a Golden Globe. 1990's police thriller *Blue Steel* proved that she could carry a serious lead role, but it was followed by a series of "wife and mother" roles until 1994.

True Lies was a blockbuster spy thriller/comedy with Arnold Schwarzenegger, in which she transformed herself from a mousy secretary into a tough and sexy superspy. In 1998 she reprised her *Halloween* role as Laurie Strode twenty years later, all grown up now and an alcoholic single mom trying to teach school and keep her life under control while (still) being stalked by the unsinkable Michael Meyers.

Curtis, who now lives in Idaho with her husband and two children, also writes best-selling children's books and enjoys photography, which she has considered making a full-time career. The identity young Jamie sought is defined the best in her writing. Her books, she says, "say more about me than all the films I've ever done. When I write, I'm being me." Long ago, her mother told her "You are okay. Show them Jamie. Don't show them who they want to see."

Of Bob Brandt, Jamie said, "My stepfather, who raised me since I was a little girl, is Daddy, the one I go to with dad problems. He has always been around and supportive—a complete papa." These days the Brandts have residences in both Beverly Hills and Sun Valley, Idaho, so they're close by if any "dad problems" arise.

Hector Barrantes, stepfather of

Sarah Ferguson, Duchess of York, author, 1959

"Hector died at the age of fifty-one. . . .I didn't feel like I had lost a father, or a stepfather. I felt like I had lost a friend—my best friend."

Sarah Margaret Ferguson was born in London, England, into a military family that could trace its ancestry back to the Royal House of Stuart. Her father, Major Ronald Ferguson, was a cavalry officer who, at the end of his military career, became deputy chairman of the Guards Polo Club at Windsor and polo manager for the Prince of Wales. His wife, Susan, came from a similar background. Little Sarah, who became known to the world simply as "Fergie," grew up on the outskirts of a world of royalty, duty, and privilege, with a generous admixture of the Sport of Kings—polo.

Sarah and her older sister Jane spent their childhood in the rural area outside of London, where Sarah became a talented and competitive equestrienne at an early age. When she was 13, events on the other side of the world changed forever the course her life would take. Hector Barrantes, a major sports figure in his native Argentina, suffered the worst tragedy of his life, an automobile accident that resulted in his fracturing a leg but cost the life of his wife and unborn child. Sympathetic friends, in an effort to cheer up the grieving Hector, arranged for a vacation in Corfu. Of the many invited guests were Ronald and Susan Ferguson.

The Fergusons' life had been fairly contented, although not entirely problem free. Ronald, although possessed of a tender side that seemed to come out mostly with his children, had become so involved with his work that his wife had begun drifting away emotionally. And the handsome and charming Barrantes was there, evidently ready to re-enter the world after the previous year's misfortunes.

Despite admitting to two extramarital affairs, one with a close friend of Susan's, Ronald Ferguson never quite seemed to understand what had driven him and his wife apart and was uncooperative even after she moved out and took a London apartment. Ronald vacillated about signing the necessary legal paperwork and Barrantes refused to live openly with Susan until she'd gotten a divorce.

The children, Jane and Sarah, reacted with a maturity beyond their years. They realized that a bad marriage could have been far worse to live in than a relatively civil divorce. They tried to be supportive of both parents. Even though their mother had been the one to dissolve the marriage and leave, the girls loved her and accepted the situation as well as they could. Staying at home with their father and continuing their educations made the transition somewhat easier, although they missed their mother a great deal and were in close contact by phone even when she was out of the country.

When Jane's schooling was finished, she spent weekdays with her mother and weekends with her father and sister. Ronald and Susan conducted themselves well and never used the children as pawns, with the result that the girls' love and respect for both parents remained intact and strong.

In 1974 the divorce finally went through and Susan Ferguson and Hector Barrantes began living together openly. Since the adults had, for the most part, handled the situation like adults, when the two married in 1975, it was with the children's blessing. They were glad to see their mother happy again. Susan took nothing into her new life but herself, leaving behind many prized possessions and making no attempt to sue for custody of the children; she thought they would be happier and more settled where they were.

For the next few years, Sarah and Jane adjusted to life with Dad. A popular student, Sarah did well enough in school, but was more focused on sports and her social life than academic pursuits. Her father might have been more concerned about this had he not been preoccupied with the fact that her sister Jane had fallen in love with a young student from Australia, whom he found unsuitable. But the Ferguson women had a stubborn streak, particularly in matters of the heart, and Jane followed him to Australia against her father's wishes.

Before the next stage of her education, Sarah decided to travel. Her first stop would be Argentina, where her mother and Hector Barrantes were living. Barrantes had been a rugby player and Golden Gloves heavyweight boxer as well as a world-class polo player.

The Barrantes owned a ranch stocked with horses, which Sarah, an accomplished horsewoman, enjoyed enormously. Their eventual goal was to own a "polo centre" where they could breed and train their own ponies. The three of them had a great time riding around in Hector's pickup truck scouting suitable locations for this future ranch. Sarah loved this time with her mother, enjoyed riding the finest polo ponies in the world, and flirted with the spirited ranch hands.

Aside from their love of polo, Barrantes and Ronald Ferguson seemed to have little in common. Ferguson had frequently preferred the company of his horses, his mother, or other women to that of his wife, whereas Barrantes considered Susan the love of his life.

"When you're happy you've always got more to give, not only to your partner but to everyone," Susan said. "I told this to Sarah and it is something she has always remembered."

Realizing that this new happier version of her mother was, at least in part, a result of the relationship with Barrantes, Sarah began to build a rapport with her stepfather.

Back in England, Sarah enrolled at Queen's Secretarial College for a two-year course, which struck her as deadly boring after her six months in Argentina. As usual, she was more inventive at finding ways to avoid schoolwork than anything else, and managed to conduct a lively social life. Before settling down to a life of secretarial work, Sarah and a friend decided to travel the world.

Again, her first stop was Argentina, where Hector and Susan were well on their way to making their dreams come true: they had purchased a 4000 acre ranch called El Pucara ("The Fortress") and were producing some of the most sought-after polo mounts in the country, if not the world. El Pucara was another world, separated by 20 miles from the nearest town and in contact with the outside world only by radio telephone. Nevertheless, as best she could, Susan had turned the place into a little corner of England on the pampas.

In the meanwhile, Ronald Ferguson had remarried and the family was growing. Sarah befriended her new stepmother (also named Susan) and became godmother to their second child.

But this settled lifestyle eluded Sarah herself, and she became part of a "jet set" crowd described as "fast, sophisticated, and possessed of a wit that can at times be biting." Through Princess Diana, she became acquainted with Prince Andrew, younger son of Queen Elizabeth, and learned that the rules all change when royalty is involved.

Freewheeling "Fergie" kept their budding romance a secret for months. Andrew's brother, Charles, the Prince of Wales, had simply ceased all association with any woman who talked publicly about their relationship, and she had no intention of letting that happen to her. The only person who was in on the secret was, or course, Princess Diana, whom she had met at the Barrantes' home earlier. Hector and Charles were both polo aficionados, and Diana and Fergie discovered that they, too, had a lot in common.

Throughout the decade and a half of their marriage, Susan Barrantes traveled all over the world with her husband, depending upon where the polo season took him. Part of the year was always spent in England and Sarah was a frequent visitor to Argentina, so the family stayed fairly intact. When Sarah and Andrew married, she and Susan were in constant contact, and Susan came back to England to attend the wedding, where she managed to clash with both her ex-husband and the press. She decided she much preferred Argentina and returned as soon as she was able.

A few years later, while in a meeting regarding one of her favorite charities, Sarah received an urgent phone call from her mother in Argentina informing her that Hector had been diagnosed with cancer of the lymph glands and would be receiving treatment in the United States. By this time Sarah was well able to balance her feelings and her duties. After asking a few pointed questions of one of the doctors in attendance, she put the disconcerting news behind her for the moment and went off to acquaint herself with more particulars of Motor Neurone Disease. As soon as she could, she flew to New York to be with her stepfather, leaving her small daughter behind.

By 1990, Hector's condition had deteriorated to the point that doctors were giving him only weeks to live. As none of the royal family had visited Argentina since the Falklands War, Sarah had to request permission from the Queen. This necessitated missing various State functions and not being able to see her husband off on his upcoming tour of sea duty, but Sarah was adamant and the Queen agreed.

For a time it seemed that Hector's condition was improving, and he was able to drive around the ranch with Sarah and Susan and enjoy the presence of his granddaughters Beatrice and Eugenie. Two days later, Hector Barrantes was dead at age 51. Susan was totally distraught by the loss but still chose to remain in Argentina.

Sarah's last memories of Hector Barrantes are of a talk they had two days before his death, in which he asked that she look after her mother, whom he loved more than anyone. He also told her to stay with her husband Andrew, whom he considered to be a good man, and not to allow herself to be trapped in any situation she would regret later. As it turned out, these requests were mutually exclusive, and she and Andrew eventually ended their marriage.

Hector's passing left his wife, and eventually his stepdaughter, with a load of debt both would struggle to pay off. Part of the ranch was sold immediately and the remainder eventually fell to the government's central bank when Argentina experienced a severe economic downturn. In order to generate funds, Sarah pulled political strings and her mother did everything from start a television production company to writing well-received books about the sport of polo.

Hector's memorial service was scheduled for the same day that Sarah was to move her family into a new house, all of which took place while her husband was away at sea. Nevertheless, she drove two hours to the site and participated in the service. "I missed Hector terribly," she said. "[But] I agreed with the American Indians—that if you lived fully, any day was a good day to die." Hector Barrantes certainly lived his life to the fullest and left his mark on those around him.

Sarah subsequently lent her name and voice to many cancer prevention organizations, frequently mentioning, as a source of her awareness "My stepfather, Hector Barrantes, whom I adored." A parent could have no better epitaph.

Paul Aaron, stepfather of

KEANU REEVES, actor, 1964

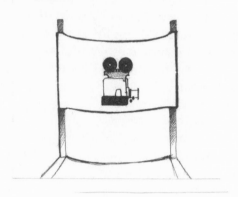

He was Keanu's stepfather for less than a year, but stayed in touch and put him in touch with the right people to help his career.

Keanu Charles Reeves was born in Beirut in 1964, the child of an English theatrical designer, Patricia, and a Chinese-Hawaiian geologist, Samuel Nowlin Reeves. In a kind of reverse East-meets-West, the London-trained Patricia had been working as a nightclub showgirl and Samuel, of the exotic mixed heritage, held a lucrative enough job with an oil company to afford a large house with servants. By the time Keanu (which means "cool breeze over the mountains") was four, they'd had his sister, Kim, and moved as far away as possible from the increasingly volatile Middle East, staying briefly in Australia before landing in New York City.

New York proved unlucky for the marriage. Before long, Samuel headed back to Hawaii. Patricia remained in New York after the divorce, but never quite came to terms with the city, which she considered to be congested, dirty and noisy. All it had to recommend it was a high level of culture and artistry, and a big enough theatrical world to enable her to resume her original profession of costume design and to meet her second husband. Paul Aaron was a relatively new stage and screen director. Keanu was about six when they married.

Patricia needed a locale that would provide a compromise between unorthodoxy and stability. Except for the weather, Toronto seemed ideal. But once again, Patricia's marriage couldn't survive a change of venue, and a year later she and Aaron divorced. Luckily for Keanu, another of the patterns in his mother's life was that she seemed able to maintain amicable enough relationships with her former husbands, who each had their own kinds of influence on the boy.

Paul Aaron stayed in touch while he was earning a reputation that would someday make him very helpful to Keanu's career. Aaron had graduated from Bennington College in Vermont, and then went off to Los Angeles to be the Casting and New Programs Director for the Mark Taper Forum, which opened on April 9, 1967. In 1969, he directed the national company of *The Prime of Miss Jean Brodie*, which starred Kim Hunter. He returned to New York to direct an off-Broadway play and then became the youngest director in Broadway history, in January 1970, with the comedy, *Paris is Out*, which ran for ninety-six performances.

He directed a play in Amsterdam, the Netherlands, and then returned again to New York. After less than ten years as a director, his work in a 1974 Broadway play was termed by *Variety*, the entertainment daily, to be "nothing less than masterful." When he went back to California, his direction of the stage play, *The Tenth Man*, starring Richard Dreyfuss, won him the Los Angeles Drama Critic's Award as Director of the Year.

His work in films was laudable as well. The NBC television special, *The Miracle Worker*, in 1979, earned him at least four awards, and the film itself won several for itself and its cast and crew.

In the 1970s, Keanu was showing himself to be not much of a scholar, due partly to dyslexia and partly to a dreamy, detached nature that also kept him from forming many close relationships at the series of schools he attended. Despite his developing into a true Canadian hockey fanatic and a talented goalie, the most important people in his life were his mother, father, and stepfathers.

Even after his mother married for the third time, Keanu managed fairly regular visits with both his father and Paul Aaron for several years. Then, when he was 13. Samuel Reeves simply and completely disappeared. For the next ten years, he made no attempt to communicate with his children, Keanu and Kim; a police search turned up no sign of him. By the time he resurfaced, the damage had been done to them. In 1994 he received a 10-year jail sentence for cocaine possession and remained out of his children's lives.

Keanu led a life that looked fairly normal on the outside but was painful on the inside. The abrupt and mysterious departure of his father from his life left him feeling isolated and alone, no matter how much his parents tried to include him in grown-up activities.

Patricia began working again as a costume designer and soon branched out into working for the bands that her rock-and-roll promoter husband associated with. During this period, Keanu not only attended every type of concert from country to rock with his parents and their friends, he also socialized with houseguests ranging from Dolly Parton to Alice Cooper. Still, something was missing, and he blamed it on his father, at one point going so far as to say, "I think a lot of who I am is a reaction against his actions."

At some point in his high school years, a new interest crept into the life of this budding jock with dreams of becoming a Toronto Maple Leaf. Perhaps vacations spent with Paul Aaron on various movie sets had exerted an unrealized influence. After winning a part in a high school production of *The Crucible*, Reeves realized that hockey was no longer going to be the main focus of his life. His mother, noting the reaction of teenage girls in the audience, allowed him to switch schools. He set his sights on Toronto's High School for the Performing Arts and, despite strong competition, won the opportunity to go there.

Keanu's focus became theater. "Then, like everything else he does, that became his sole abiding interest," Paul Aaron is quoted as saying. "I mean, every part of it—the voice, the movement, the contemporary, the classical." Keanu worked overtime to learn the techniques and gained working experience in whatever spare time he had, doing commercials, TV walk-ons, whatever came along.

Upon leaving school, he did more work in Toronto theater, but eventually realized that his future lay in Hollywood. His mother supported his decision and Paul Aaron was more than willing to help. Keanu could live with him until he got situated, and Aaron had already started lining up introductions to the right people.

One of these was Erwin Stoff, and Keanu's career is one of those that Stoff is managing with his 3 Arts Entertainment. He found Keanu an agent, who was so personally taken with him that she was sending him out on auditions immediately. Made-for-TV as well as big-screen movies began coming his way. Paul Aaron even co-produced some of them.

Keanu's interim stepfather, but lifelong mentor, is a jack of all trades, who has written, directed and produced for Broadway, television and film. His television and Hollywood movies extended all the way from Chuck Norris kick-em-ups to the Emmy-winning life story of Helen Keller. There were action movies, thrillers and love stories, all which are standard show business genres.

Yet many of them had a kind of twist that set them apart. Perhaps a key to Aaron's work is that there is frequently a little more than meets the eye, something quirky, hidden or unusual. A late 70's romance called *A Different Story*, told the tale of a gay man and a lesbian, who married for convenience and then fell in love—perhaps not a very likely premise, but who was making even remotely gay-themed movies at that time?

In the 1980s, he was doing Broadway, television specials, and films. On the one hand, he has been supportive of actors since he began an actors' workshop in 1969, and on the other hand, he is President of Elsboy Entertainment, which was involved with both management and production. Elsboy now concentrates on the latter, while management is with a former working partner, Erwin Stoff.

1987's *In Love and War* was not just a POW/war story: the captured Navy pilot knew the truth about the Gulf of Tonkin incident, which was the basis for our entry into the Vietnam War (shades of Oliver Stone) and kept silent through years of torture. In 1995 Aaron directed a movie called *Maxie*, in which a 1920's flapper reincarnates briefly and enlivens a marriage with her vibrant, sexy presence.

Aaron's aim was always to make people look past the surface, finding the truth wherever it lay. In a 1984 TV movie, *When She Says No*, he told the story of a rape from four different points of view and then left the audience to draw some of its own conclusions, which some might find irritating from an artistic point of view, but is undoubtedly the way events frequently play out in real life.

In 1995, he and Robert Redford worked together to produce an HBO mini-series about three Native American families, which followed a television series about an African-American family, starring James Earl Jones, and preceded his work to develop a series about a Cuban-American family.

A 1999 Miramax film, *In Too Deep*, which he both wrote and produced, dealt with moral ambiguity in the life of an undercover cop who became deeply enmeshed in the Cincinnati drug culture. In pursuit of realism, Aaron spent seven years researching this venture, interviewing countless people. The director he chose, Michael Rymer, echoed Aaron's sentiments when he said, "With any films about human beings and human relationships, you must always transcend the surface of things." Aaron obviously wanted the audience to wander the gray areas and gain some understanding of the complexity of human behavior rather than simply present a run-of-the-mill cops and robbers movie.

In one notable case, Aaron requested that his name be removed from a film he had directed, an unusual but not unknown occurrence. The Directors Guild only allows this after the formal process of appeal to the Guild, and then only if a film has been altered far beyond the original intent by someone other than the person who is named as its director. The 1987 film *Morgan Stewart's Coming Home* listed as Director: "Alan

Smithee replacing Paul Aaron." The Directors Guild had sanctioned the use of a code name that would signify to those in the know that a particular project had been disowned by its director. The name Alan Smithee was thought to be unusual enough that it would never have to be replaced, assuming no real Alan Smithee existed. It is unclear from the outside what led Aaron to be "replaced" by Smithee. Perhaps he simply thought along the same lines as his stepson, who is quoted as saying, "When I don't feel free and can't do what I want I just react. I go against it."

Just as his stepfather worked in all media from farce to high drama, live and film, Keanu Reeves has run the gamut of characters on stage and screen, from the goofiness of the Bill and Ted movies to Shakespeare, frequently citing *Romeo & Juliet's* Mercutio as his favorite role. Although catapulted to fame via the action romance *Speed*, he also accepted, and shone in, offbeat roles in such productions as *Wolfboy*, a 1984 play in which he portrayed a suicidal teenager victimized by a male prostitute, and a 1991 movie, *My Own Private Idaho*, where he himself played a male prostitute, half of a wandering duo of outcast misfits who roamed the world looking for love and respect—or as close as they could get to it. In Roger Ebert's words, "The achievement of this film is that it wants to evoke that state of drifting need, and it does. There is no mechanical plot that has to grind to a Hollywood conclusion, and no contrived test for the heroes to pass; this is a movie about two particular young men, and how they pass their lives."

The truth is what is—look at it and draw your own conclusions. But *look*. Use words like odd, depressing, unbelievable, if you will, but *look*. Perhaps Keanu was drawn to such parts because of something he absorbed from Paul Aaron.

Steve Bennett, stepfather of

LUKE PERRY, actor, ca 1966

"[T]he greatest man I know. I love him. I wish he was my real father. He's the one who taught me the important things I needed to know about being a man."

Luke Perry was born Coy Luther Perry III in Mansfield, Ohio, on October 11, 1966—as far as anyone knows. The star of Fox Network's popular show *Beverly Hills 90210*, cautioned by his employers not to reveal his true age for fear of losing pre-teenage fans, has left such a trail of obfuscation that his real birth date is pretty much anyone's guess, but his mother's.

Luke grew up in Fredericktown, Ohio, and wanted to be an actor ever since he knew what the word meant. When Luke was six, his parents divorced, and he never saw his father, until his father's funeral eight years later. When Luke was twelve, Mrs. Perry married Steve Bennett, a construction worker, who enjoyed taking Luke and his brother to work with him and teaching the boys about the construction business.

Luke feels himself to be far more a child of the Midwest than of Hollywood. "The best friends of my life come from that small town," he said. "Some of the best people who I know are there. I call them all the time." At Fredericktown High School, which offered classes on animal husbandry and taught driver's ed students how to drive tractors, Luke was popular, but a scholastically indifferent student who got into a lot of mischief and was voted Biggest Flirt by his senior class. He played baseball and tennis and had his first "acting" role as Freddie Bird, the Fredericktown football mascot. On one memorable occasion, Luke made a spectacular entrance in a helicopter rented from his stepfather's company. The helicopter lit on the field and out jumped Luke in yellow tights, red plumes, a cape, and huge webbed feet!

Success did not come overnight. Luke counted at least 216 unsuccessful auditions before he finally secured a role on a soap opera in 1987. The show was called *Loving*, and Luke portrayed an amiable country boy, which one can imagine was not too much of a stretch. Luke moved first to New York, then to Hollywood, where he did menial work ranging from shoe salesman to short order cook. His background in construction may have helped him land several jobs on construction and road crews. At one time, he worked on the parking lot at Torrance High School, which coincidentally became the set for *Beverly Hills 90210*.

The popularity of *Beverly Hills 90210*, and the volume of Luke Perry's fan mail, shot through the roof. Personal appearances turned into riots, and Luke found himself in the position of contacting hospitalized victims of the mob violence to express his regret. This surely was a side of show business that the Ohio farm boy found hard to deal with. Luke describes himself as "not ultra-cool," drives a used car, and shares his leased house with a potbellied pig named Jerry Lee, after his favorite rock star. Rather than attend trendy gyms, he has a punching bag in his yard, and rides a dirt bike for fun. Luke ascribes his values to his stepfather, "the greatest man I know. I love him. I wish he was my real father. He's the one who taught me the important things I needed to know about being a man."

John Bickford, stepfather of

JEFF GORDON, race car driver, 1971

"I have great parents who gave me the opportunities
to be a race car driver. . .the way it's all worked out. . .
makes [them] heroes in my mind."

Considered by many to be the best race car driver of all times, Jeff Gordon was born in Vallejo, California, the second child of Carol and Will Gordon. They divorced when Jeff was a baby and Carol married John Bickford, who worked in the auto parts business and was a lifelong racing fan. In fact, on their first date, he took her to the Vallejo Speedway.

Jeff's racing career began with BMX bikes, which many neighborhood kids rode on a dirt track near their house. Despite helmets and full padding, the sport produced a lot of accidents and made Jeff''s mother extremely nervous—her boy was only four years old, one of the youngest on the track. Jeff rode with training wheels until Bickford threatened to take the bike to the dump if he didn't learn to ride it properly. He mastered the bike in one afternoon.

Nevertheless, Carol wanted Jeff out of bike racing. Bickford's response to this was to buy his stepson a quarter midget race car, not exactly what Mom had in mind, but she soon decided this was safer than bike racing.

Jeff loved the car: a three horsepower open-cockpit racer with roll cage, in which the driver wears a seat belt, harness and helmet. Five-year-old Jeff and his stepfather built a race track in a field near their home and he practiced every day. Jeff was a natural and was soon racing at local tracks. Bickford bought the boy an official racing uniform and made him learn to dress himself without help, so he would develop a proper racing mindset.

Bickford discouraged Jeff from forming close relationships with other young drivers, fearing it would dull his competitive edge. "Decisions weren't based on emotion," he said. "They were all based on logic. I have a cold personality. I'm not a hugger. I'm a guy who looks at it, attacks it, tries to succeed....I approached [Jeff's development as a racer] from a professional standpoint. This wasn't about having fun. If we want to have fun, we'll go to Disney World."

At age eight, Jeff won his first quarter midget championship. The next step was ten horsepower go-karts. For the next few years he competed in both types of races, frequently pretending to be Luke Skywalker in his X-wing fighter. The Force was with him: he won so often against older, more experienced drivers that he was suspected of being a twenty-year-old in a clever disguise.

Bickford celebrated (and advertised) by having "Jeff Gordon" t-shirts made up, which he sold for twelve dollars apiece. At age ten, Jeff won every race he entered, all against much older drivers. "My father was building a future star," he said. "I was just having fun."

But the fun didn't last forever. After months of traveling all over the state with Jeff's racer loaded in the back of Bickford's truck, in which they slept to save money, Jeff began to burn out. Even Luke Skywalker needs a vacation now and then.

They took a summer off and Jeff learned to water ski. But between his natural desire to please his second father and his own love of racing, Jeff was soon back, driving bigger and better cars than ever.

At twelve, Jeff was driving a 600 hp sprint car that he and his father built out of whatever parts they could find. With the same open cockpit as a midget but many times the horsepower, sprint cars were considered one of the most dangerous vehicles to drive. For that reason, sprint drivers had to be at least sixteen years old to compete in California. The innovative Jeff grew as much of a mustache as he could at his age, darkened it with an eyebrow pencil, and sneaked into as many races as he could. Racing was sometimes a struggle, and after crashing on a wet track, Jeff was even tempted to quit, but Bickford wouldn't hear of it.

Having learned during their travels that many Midwestern tracks had no age restrictions, Bickford decided to sell his business and move the entire family to Indiana. Jeff's obvious talent, and Bickford's vision for his future, was now the driving force in their lives—a bad pun, perhaps, but also the truth. Jeff won his first sprint car race in Ohio later that year. His father was so elated that he ran down to the track, lifted Jeff up in his arms, and hugged him while they both had a good cry. Bickford, evidently, wasn't all business, all the time. But he was walking a tightrope in one respect. "I always wanted to race," he said, "but I couldn't afford it. I was living my dreams through Jeff. . .I taught him the only thing I knew, how to race." The time would come when this over-identification of his own dreams with his child's would boomerang on him.

At sixteen, Jeff got his driver's license the same day he got his United States Automobile Club license, the youngest driver ever to attain that distinction. Ironically he had already won over 100 races before even taking a driver's education class.

In the course of his career, it would be hard to keep track of all the "youngests," "mosts," and "bests" attached to Jeff's name in the record books. He missed out on a lot of normal teenage social activities due to racing obligations, but was popular enough to be voted prom king at Tri-West High School in Pittsboro, Indiana. Jeff insists that he doesn't regret a thing.

Then it was time to decide what course his future would take. After discussing it with his parents, he realized that college didn't seem like an option and the Indy car circuit would be too difficult to get into without sponsorship. A more logical course suggested itself: Bickford would arrange for Jeff to attend Buck Baker's driving school in Rockingham, N.C.

The first time Jeff drove a stock car, there was no doubt in his mind what he wanted to do with the rest of his life. He loved the feel of the big cars, their power, the way they handled—he was hooked. Jeff and his father found someone who would sponsor his entry into the Busch Grand National circuit, a sort of entry level NASCAR tour. Within a year he had been discovered by a top-level management team and signed on with Hendrick Motorsports to compete for the Winston Cup, racing's most prestigious award.

Jeff and his parents moved to Charlotte, N.C., where Hendrick was located. During the next three years, Jeff built up an impressive record. There is a complicated system for amassing championship points, involving not only winning races, but also leading individual laps and completing the most laps in a race. Points are added up and at the end of the season, and the top 25 drivers receive cash prizes. Jeff was blowing them away in all categories and in 1995 won his first Winston Cup.

By this time, he was married to a former Miss Winston, Brooke Sealey. Jeff felt the need to break free from his parents and assert himself. "I felt like I was almost being treated like a little boy," he said. In 1995 he hired a professional business manager.

His stepfather not only felt wounded by this decision, but was left high and dry without employment, after having put all his occupational and financial eggs into the Jeff Gordon basket two decades before.

John Bickford seemed to have recovered enough to speak highly of his stepson in a 2003 interview at the Indianapolis Motor Speedway. Jeff was participating in an exhibition race where he would drive a Formula One car for the first time.

"America needs a Formula One driver," Bickford said. "There's a kid out there in America someplace that can do this. And that kid can be a Jeff Gordon or a Mario Andretti and he can compete at a level that he represents America in Victory Lane."

Jeff Gordon was not only a winner on the track, he was just what the image-driven sponsors dreamed about as a representative of the sport: handsome, clean-cut, and just the right combination of humble and confident. Modern pro sports have become a combination of athletic prowess and show business, and charisma is often a factor equal to talent. Jeff was the only race driver ever to be represented by the William Morris Talent Agency, has appeared regularly on The Late Show, and endorses everything from Quaker State Motor Oil to Edy's Ice Cream. On the more serious side, he is known for donating a large portion of his winnings to charity and participating in many educational programs for children. His motto—and the theme of his own life in racing—is "Don't Ever Quit."

Philip "Sarge" Harrison, stepfather of

SHAQUILLE O'NEAL, basketball player, 1972

"If it hadn't been for Phil, I'm not sure what would have happened to me. . . [but] my father prepared me for anything."

It's telling that in most of what is written by or about him, Shaquille O'Neal never refers to his mother's husband, Phil Harrison, as anything other than "Dad," "my father," occasionally "Sarge," or, rarely, "Phil." He is never "my stepfather." Mom and Dad are the two people who raised him together from the age of two, and, in Shaquille's words, "made me a man."

Phil Harrison and Lucille O'Neal met about two years after Shaquille was born and married shortly thereafter. Harrison called it love at first sight, claiming that "The whole block just lit up when I saw her."

Lucille was more pragmatic. "I think a father in the household is extra, a luxury," she said. "It's good if you've got a man, but if you don't have one, then you go on and you work with what you've got." She did not regard Harrison as a knight in shining armor come to rescue her and young Shaquille

Rashaun (Islamic for "Little Warrior"), but there is no indication that their union was anything but happy, having lasted into the present and produced three more children.

At first both Lucille and Phil worked for the City of Newark New Jersey, but to earn more money, Phil decided to make the military his career and enlisted in the army. At times he worked two additional jobs to support his growing family. That meant he spent a lot of time away from home, but when he was there, he made his presence known.

Both Shaquille and his mother admit that Shaq was somewhat spoiled as a young child and was all boy: mischievous, curious, and apt to do about anything if the notion struck him, including setting fire to a toy teddy bear just to see what would happen. What happened was a room filled with smoke and a solid "butt-whoopin'." This was not an isolated incident, and as Shaquille grew up, he graduated from pranks to what he candidly refers to as simply being a bully.

The family was neither affluent nor poverty stricken, due in no small part to Phil's strong work ethic and sense of discipline. But family stability was not helped by the frequent moves necessitated by his various army postings, and the Harrisons spent the next ten years living all over New Jersey, in Georgia, and finally Germany.

Young Shaquille learned to get along with an ever-changing mix of classmates of all races and backgrounds, and was taught by his parents that people are more realistically divided into good and bad than black and white.

The same could be said of Shaquille himself. An amiable kid who could be counted on to baby-sit his younger siblings, including diaper duty, Shaquille nevertheless seemed to be in constant trouble of one sort or another.

He was a bright child who skipped first grade entirely, and maintains that he did poorly in school, not because of Attention Deficit Disorder, as his teachers claimed, but simply because he was bored silly and always looking for ways to amuse himself and others.

Often the butt of jokes aimed at his size, he sometimes clowned around in hopes of gaining acceptance by making his classmates laugh. But the older he got, the more apt he was to answer their taunts with a smack in the head.

This did not go unnoticed by his father, whose theory was that Shaquille should just block out the jeers and buckle down. Education was more important than revenge. He should take pride in himself, even if he did feel "different," and if he learned to respect himself, respect for others would naturally follow. His basic message was, "Be focused, be cool." The other, perhaps contradictory, part of the message was, "And if you don't, I'll beat your butt."

But there was no contradiction in Phil Harrison. Faced with the necessity of disciplining an unruly and very large child, he saw nothing wrong with backing up the force of his personality with the force of his good right arm. After Shaq set off a fire alarm on the army base, Phil came after Shaq with a racquetball paddle, but usually the hand (or fist) was empty. Although eventually it all worked. The first ten years or so of their relationship had its share of conflict.

Shaquille states frequently that he considered himself to be a follower rather than a leader, and that he did not always pick his leaders wisely. The rowdy crowds he associated with usually limited their youthful iniquities to vandalism and petty theft, some of which might have been motivated by Shaquille's admitted resentment of the luxuries the officers' children had that he did not. Indeed, enlisted personnel were sometimes forced onto food stamps.

The one problem Shaquille didn't have was substance abuse. Booze tasted "nasty," drugs were dangerous, and worst of all, getting caught with either would incur the wrath of his dad.

A persistent rumor among army brats was that repeated misbehavior would result in being sent back to the USA. Shaq tried his best to find out if this were true. Finally Phil put an end to the shenanigans by simply declaring that he would *NEVER* send or permit Shaq to be sent home under *ANY* circumstances, and what's more, would deliver *ALL* the punishment necessary to make sure the boy paid attention.

When he was about thirteen, a couple of events seem to have sent Shaquille's life, and the relationship with his stepfather, into a different direction. Shaquille had gotten caught in a vicious circle of teasing another boy in one of his classes. The boy then told on him, which aggravated Shaquille into throwing things at the boy, who then reported him again—and around and around they went. Shaquille decided to put an end to it by waylaying the kid after class and giving him a sound beating. To his horror, the boy began having seizures. Luckily, someone on the scene knew what to do and the incident didn't end as badly as it could have. The light blinked on for Shaquille as he realized he could easily have killed someone.

Phil once told his son that he beat him because he simply didn't listen to anything. Now he began to listen. The beatings ceased and became man-to-man talks. About everything.

Shaquille was no overnight saint. He still ran with his wild friends, but some balance was being established. He was listening to another voice. At one point, when the gang decided to not merely break into a car and lift the contents, but to steal the car itself, Shaquille decided they had simply gone too far. Something told him he shouldn't be present for this one, even though his friends called him names and went right on without him. This time the gang's luck ran out and they were caught. Had he stayed, it would not have been a basketball court, but another kind of court, and stripes instead of stardom.

Shaquille attributes his change of attitude to his father's discipline finally sinking in—he was internalizing Sarge's lessons and thinking for himself. Shaquille draws a clear line in his own mind between punishment and abuse. When he misbehaved and got caught, Sarge punched him out. End of story. As long as he felt his father's motivation was "to straighten me out," he could accept the punishment and even love the man dishing it out.

Where was Lucille O'Neal Harrison while all this was going on? What did she think of the sometimes contentious relationship between her husband and her adored son? Having once sent a crying and defeated Shaquille back outside to deal with the kid who'd bested him, she was not one to tolerate what she considered weakness, and proudly refers to her son's having inherited "Phil's no-nonsense toughness."

128

Phil's take on it was that although he might occasionally beat on his son, he loved him and knew when to stop. If Shaq's bad attitude got him in trouble on the street, he could get killed. Besides, he'd been raised that way by his Jamaican father and he had turned out to be a responsible man, though not before he had wasted a lot of time in pursuits ranging from youthful craziness to downright gangsterism. He doesn't elaborate much on this aspect of his life, but it certainly gave him a high level of resolve that his children weren't going to be like him in that respect.

Somewhere along the way, the military model became Phil Harrison's blueprint for life. He adopted General Patton's philosophy that it was more important to be respected than to be loved; the love would come later when they realized that the discipline he'd taught them had saved their lives in combat. That was the way it worked with Shaquille and Phil.

Life with Sarge wasn't a constant round of crime and punishment, although some of his teaching methods might be considered unorthodox at best. He and Shaquille shared a lifelong love of sports. According to Shaquille's grandmother, he was born to play ball, and from an early age, always had either a football or a basketball in his hands. Phil, who had played some kind of ball all his life on various neighborhood or army teams, tried to give his son a solid background in sports, even coaching some of the base teams Shaq played on.

Noting that the boy tended to cringe when he saw a hard-launched football coming at him, Phil's solution was to throw the ball directly into Shaquille's face. The pain was fleeting, Shaq admitted, and never as bad as the anticipation of pain.

Although Shaquille eventually concentrated on basketball, he maintains that he has "good hands" because of Phil, and believes that the combination of Phil and sports got him through his teens. But what he remembers the most was the simple lessons of hard work, concentration and persistence. And toughness.

"You love this ball,' Phil always told him, "because someday this ball is going to put food on your table." Much later, executives with the Orlando Magic would call Shaquille "instinctively level headed" and the hardest working player on the team. Shaquille would surely attribute this to his first coach, Phil Harrison.

Shaquille says Phil has mellowed with the years, and now calls him to intercede in problem situations involving his younger siblings. But having said that, he adds that he's glad Phil hadn't "gone soft" yet when he was a kid.

Shaquille's biological father, Joe Toney, dismissed by his mother as nothing but a "sperm donor," surfaced briefly from time to time, but certainly played no permanent part in his son's life. Phil, who knew Toney from Newark, reports having a conversation with him in which he calmly relinquished any interest in Shaquille—he had a new son and no time for any of the others (apparently he had several children). Later, after Toney attempted to cash in on Shaquille's growing popularity, his son retaliated with a withering attack delivered via one track on a rap album, in which he not very politely invited Toney to get lost—he already had a father.

As a grown man, who had become both an actor and a basketball star, Shaquille O'Neal bought his parents a new house and proudly presented his father with the keys to a luxury automobile. But, true to his upbringing, he knew that material things, while nice, weren't the whole story. Shaquille gave his first basketball championship ring to the man who made it all possible, Phil Harrison. It was a symbol of his love and respect for the man he called Dad.

Harry Robinson, stepfather of

VINCE CARTER, basketball player, 1977

"My parents are my inspiration. Believe it or not,
they're my personal coaches. After every game
I still call them and get their take on how I played."

Vince Carter is what you might call a triple threat: great athlete, talented musician, and dedicated philanthropist. Add to that the fact that his compatriots almost uniformly judge him to be an all around nice guy and you have someone who stands out even in the rarefied atmosphere of the NBA. Reportedly able to dribble a basketball at age two, it was no surprise that he eventually turned to pro sports. But the rest of Vince Carter's early life didn't progress as smoothly as his unfolding court talent.

After years of arguing and unpleasantness, his parents divorced when Vince was seven years old. Not long after, Vince's mother, a teacher, developed an interest in a fellow teacher. She and Harry Robinson married. Harry was a good fit. Life became calmer and more stable, and Vince and his brother came to consider Harry Robinson their father in every sense of the word.

The Robinsons' first task was to convince Vince that there was more to life than basketball. Vince's favorite players were Julius Erving and his uncle, Oliver Lee, who for a time played for the Chicago Bulls. Uncle Oliver taught Vince a lot about basketball, but his stepfather led him into another direction entirely: music. Without giving up basketball (he could jump so high the other kids called him UFO), Vince was able to both concentrate on his studies and begin learning various musical instruments. Harry Robinson was the band director and encouraged Vince to try a little bit of everything to see what he liked.

Vince liked it all: alto sax, tenor sax, trumpet and drums. Drums were great: he could physically pour all his energy into them, and because he was setting the beat, it gave him the feeling that he was in control of the entire band. Vince liked being out in front to the extent that he even became the drum major for the high school marching band, as well as writing the homecoming theme song which the band performed.

Not only did he play in the marching band from age twelve, Vince still played all kinds of sports: volleyball, tennis, track, and football, where he was versatile enough to play both offense and defense. As might be expected, he played quarterback. He liked to be the leader.

The Robinsons always knew Vince could be a basketball great, ever since he used to follow his mother around on shopping trips dribbling an imaginary basketball. But they insisted that he be two things: a well-rounded person, and an individual.

Vince had actually been cut from the high school basketball team at age fourteen for being too little and too slow. He suddenly grew six inches in height and began developing, turning into a good offensive player. He became a point guard because that put him in charge of setting up the plays. Vince seemed to be a born leader and was recruited heavily during his senior year.

The next step was choosing a college. Vince decided in favor of the University of North Carolina, whose coach seemed most interested in impressing him with the school's fine academic program. At that level, he was playing with the best players from all over the country and so he saw relatively little court time. This motivated him to work even harder to stand out. By his junior year he was named to the All-Atlantic Coast conference and as a second team All-American. He was frequently compared to Michael Jordan.

The pressure to enter the NBA draft was enormous, but on the other hand, Vince was enjoying his stay at UNC, where he was a popular campus personality and a good student, well on his way to earning a degree in African-American studies.

This was something to talk over with the people who mattered most to him: his basketball coach and his parents. Their advice was the same as always: be yourself, follow your dream, know your own mind and act on its dictates. Vince decided on the NBA, but true to his promise to his mother, he returned in the off-seasons to finish his college degree.

Vince expected his first year in the NBA to be like his first year in college—take it slow, learn the game. But it was a difficult time in the NBA. Vince's team, the newly established Toronto Raptors, were dealing with the aftermath of a players' strike and the departure of their general manager, coach, and star player. There was a huge gap to be filled in this emerging franchise, and it fell to Vince to help pull the Raptors up out of obscurity.

He had one of the best first seasons of all times, racking up such impressive statistics that he won two separate Rookie of the Year titles and was the only rookie to lead his team in scoring. By his second year, he was such a consistently high scorer that no one doubted his future in the NBA.

Vince Carter is known as much for his winning personality as for his winning statistics. In the cutthroat atmosphere of upper echelon pro sports, Vince was uniformly considered a "nice guy," who was always willing to give teammates credit for helping him achieve as much as he did. In fact, that was the other side of the comparison to Michael Jordan: although their styles were technically similar, Vince lacked what some termed Jordan's "killer instinct," and found that an obstacle to his rise to the absolute pinnacle of NBA stardom.

Therefore, the 2000 Olympic Games were a surprise to a lot of people. Personal troubles ranging from a dishonest agent causing financial problems to the breakup of his parents' marriage seemed to bring out a more aggressive side of him that some characterized as "an arrogant bully."

After the Olympics, he regained his equilibrium, but kept some of the new toughness he had acquired. During the 2000 playoffs, Carter emerged as a truly dazzling presence on the court. Even so, he left during the series to attend his college graduation, keeping the promise he had made to his parents six years before.

No matter where he played, traveled or lived, Carter always remained rooted in the life and culture of Daytona Beach, Florida, where he grew up. The year his mother retired from teaching, Vince donated $10,000 to his alma mater, Mainland High School, to be used by both their sports and music programs.

Not content with simply contributing a little here and there, Vince (with the cooperation of his entire family) eventually founded Embassy of Hope Foundation. Both parents served as officers in the non-profit organization, which provides holiday food baskets and Christmas parties for needy families, summer basketball camps, a variety of activities aimed at encouraging young people to stay in school and complete their education, and much more. In the works is a project tentatively titled Vince's Village, a haven for abused children

Vince worked hard to provide funds for the foundation, devoting much of his off-season time to fund-raising events such as golf tournaments, baseball games, and celebrity auctions — and all of this while doing work toward his bachelor's degree at UNC. After all, he actually signed a contract with his mother promising that he would get that degree. And no child of Harry and Michelle Carter-Robinson would go back on a promise like that.

Kurt Russell, stepfather of

KATE HUDSON, actor, 1979

She gave her first child the middle name of Russell, after her stepfather.

Born in Los Angeles, Goldie Hawn's look-alike daughter followed her parents into show business and, like one of her better known movies, is "almost famous." Kate Hudson has already won a Golden Globe on her way to stardom.

Hawn and first husband, actor/comedian/musician Bill Hudson, divorced when their daughter was 18 months old. Since 1982, Kate and her brother were raised with actor Kurt Russell playing the role of father. A stepbrother and half-brother completed the family. Kate had little contact with her father and considers Goldie Hawn and Kurt Russell to be her parents.

Probably best known for his action/adventure movies, Kurt Russell started out as a Disney regular, starring in dozens of TV shows and movies as a youngster. His father, a former baseball player, moved to Hollywood and became an actor, and Kurt followed in his father's footsteps in almost every way, including minor league baseball. A torn rotator cuff ended that career almost before it began, and the promising young athlete with a

.400 batting average returned to show business. One of the highlights of his early career was a turn as Elvis Presley which earned him an Emmy nomination. He met and married Susan Hubley, with whom he had a son, Boston, in 1981.

Not long after his brief marriage dissolved, Russell met Goldie Hawn while filming *Swing Shift*, an unusual WWII romance set in a defense plant, with Hawn as a Rosie The Riveter, who falls in love with co-worker Russell. The couple never felt the need to marry, even after the birth of their son, but have been together for over 20 years.

Russell has played a number of tough-guy action roles in such movies as *Escape From New York*, *The Thing*, *Big Trouble in Little China*, *Escape From L.A.*, and *Soldier*, but also did noteworthy dramatic work in films such as *Silkwood* and *Backdraft*, and was able to infuse even some of his toughest characters with a degree of humanity that kept them from being caricatures.

Kate Hudson was accepted at New York University's Tisch School of the Arts, but persuaded her parents to allow her to postpone her education to search for suitable film roles. Despite belonging to a show business family, Kate acquired an agent on her own and was soon landing TV and movie roles, albeit not major ones. But no matter the level of critical acclaim or financial success of the films themselves, Kate usually garnered good reviews and was seen as having inherited what one critic called "her mother's offbeat sexiness and natural comic flair."

Her best-known and most critically acclaimed performance to date was in 2000 in *Almost Famous*, as one of a group of girls known as the "Band-Aids," camp followers of the rock bands of the 1970's. For what one critic termed her "glowing performance" as Penny Lane, Chief Groupie of a band called Stillwater, Kate received both a Golden Globe and an Oscar nomination. The much-in-demand actress capitalized on this recognition, and completed three films in 2003 alone.

Then life began to imitate art, and Kate married Chris Robinson, lead singer of a group called Black Crowes. Three years later, their first child was born and was named Ryder Russell Robinson. One suspects the middle name was chosen for love of someone and not simply for alliteration.

136

Invitation to Honor Yours

Now, if the card we put in this book at the printer fell out or became lost, here again is the invitation:

Please send your stories of wonderful stepparents or stepchildren to us with your name, address, telephone number, e-mail address.

Put the words "Wonderful Stepparent" or "Wonderful Stepchild" on the envelope or as the e-mail subject line. Yours, too, may appear in a book as did the one for our deserving Moms.

Wonderful Stepparents
Lawells Publishing
PO Box 1338
Royal Oak MI 48068
lawells@tm.net

Be sure to celebrate Stepfamily Day every September 16, brought to us by the Stepfamily Association of America, www.saafamilies.org.

Your bookstore also has:
Dedicated Dads: Stepfathers of Famous People
Fantastic Famous Stepparents

About the Author

A displaced Hoosier, who has lived in Michigan long enough to think of herself as at least an honorary Michigander, I was born long enough ago to remember owning a black-and-white television and a reel-to-reel tape recorder. The transition from rural Indiana to the Metro Detroit area caused a bit of culture shock (I had not realized that towns could be contiguous and not separated by eight miles of cornfields) but I'm fairly certain it was meant to be.

After years of working in the offices of everything from junk yards to banks, I was laid off form my job of 26 years with local furnace manufacturer, and now divide my time between working for temporary office services and freelance writing. Someday, I want to do nothing but write.

I admit to loving: dogs, the music of Rachmaninoff, The Eagles, jewel, The Judds, and Josh Groban; dogs; The Cat Who mysteries; dogs; almost anything chocolate; and, did I mention, dogs?

Rusty Hancock

About the Illustrator

Ever since I was a little girl, I've been drawing my own illustrations for my homemade books. My love of drawing brought me to Kendall College of Art & Design in Grand Rapids, Michigan in 1998 where I earned a BFA with a major in Illustration in 2002. I am pleased to be a member of the Society of Children's Book Writers and Illustrators, which directly led to my getting this project.

I enjoy spending time with my husband, Tim, in the quiet town of Zeeland, Michigan. One can find me taking long walks in the outdoors, watching classic movies or just enjoying a laugh with friends and family.

Megan Van Kampen